The Godric Cycling Club has ~~~
for many – for young and not so ~ ~ ~
as being a competitive club. In the later years the May Day Races
have brought many keen cyclists and visitors to Bungay.

I wish them well for this publication, and for many more
successful years of cycling.

Roma Went
Town Mayor of Bungay
April, 2003

It does not seem half a century ago that the founder members of the
Godric Cycling Club got together to form an organisation for
enthusiasts of the sport.

But 50 years later, in 2003, they and everyone now connected
with the club can look back with pride on an organisation that has
carried the name of Bungay throughout the country. It has attracted
riders to its events in the town from far and wide, too, and Bungay
is proud to have such a well-run and well-respected club in its midst.

I am grateful to have this opportunity to congratulate Godric on
its golden anniversary, and wish it well for the future. This book,
which traces its history from its formation in 1953, is a permanent
commemoration and a fitting tribute to the men and women who
have worked with commitment and dedication over the years to
make Godric the highly respected club it is in the cycling world in
this country today.

Terry Reeve
Town Reeve of Bungay
April, 2003

Front cover: start of a club-run, spring 1959; (left to right) Daphne and George King, Lindsay Wigby, Ronnie Harrison, Roy Pulford, 'Eddie' Edwards, Michael Ratcliff

WHEELS ALONG THE WAVENEY

WHEELS ALONG THE WAVENEY

A HISTORY OF
THE GODRIC CYCLING CLUB
1953–2003

Tim Hilton

WHEELS ALONG THE WAVENEY
A HISTORY OF THE GODRIC CYCLING CLUB 1953–2003

Copyright © Tim Hilton 2003

First published in 2003 by
Mousehold Press
Victoria Cottage
Constitution Opening
Norwich, NR3 4BD

for the Godric Cycling Club,
Bungay
Suffolk

ISBN 1 874739 27 7

Printed by Barnwells
Aylsham
Norfolk

INTRODUCTION

This short book is a history of the Godric Cycling Club and is published as part of the club's golden jubilee celebrations in 2003. Its author hopes that the volume will interest not only past and present members of the Godric C.C., but all our friends in the Waveney Valley and cyclists from further afield.

The primary sources for my narrative are in the 'Godric Scrap Books', preserved in the club's collection. There are nearly two dozen of these books. Some are full. Others are lacking in details. One or two are missing. The books were first compiled by Geoff Mayne and later taken over by Cyril Wigby. They contain newspaper cuttings, programmes of races, photographs, menus of annual dinners, general announcements to members, and continuing issues of the club's newsletter.

It is a wonderful archive but cannot provide a full record of the club's life, nor of the separate achievements of the Godric C.C. members. The present book is a general history of the club. No individual cyclist will find a complete account of his or her racing career. I thought it more important to mention very many people who have competed in the Godric colours, whether as champions or as schoolchildren.

My thanks go to the cyclists who have helped me with the book. First among them are the journalists and part-time correspondents who have reported East Anglian cycling in local newspapers; I particularly appreciate the columns written by Mick Gambling, the late Ivan Jekyll and Fergus Muir. And, of course, on the road or in the café, numerous Godrics have told me of their cycling lives. In addition, the manuscript was prepared for press by Lynda Fairbairn; and the author and the Godric C.C. owe gratitude to Adrian Bell of Mousehold Press in Norwich, who is the book's publisher.

My clubmates will agree that a history of the Godric C.C. should be dedicated, first, to the memory of the late George King, who was the club's founder; secondly, to his widow, Daphne King, who was the co-founder and still looks after the well-being of men she knew as boys; and, thirdly, to Geoff Mayne, who was one of those boys in 1953, has held practically every office in the club, has also held many of its racing records, and is now, half a century later, about to retire from his position as our Chairman.

T.H.
Uggeshall, 2003

George King

CHAPTER 1

The ancient town of Bungay is situated at a bow of the River Waveney in north Suffolk. The river forms the border between Suffolk and Norfolk. Norwich is fifteen miles to the north of Bungay, Ipswich is 35 miles to the south. To the west of Bungay we can follow the Waveney river to its source near Diss. To Bungay's east, the river flows through Beccles and Oulton Broad before it turns inland to become a part of the southern Norfolk Broads. A channel between Oulton Broad and Lowestoft connects the Waveney to the North Sea.

This natural boundary gives a character to our region far beyond the river's banks and meadows. In former times the Waveney was navigable as far upstream as Bungay and was used to transport grain, malt and other agricultural products. Bungay and Beccles have never been rich industrial towns. But neither have they been poor; and in their different ways they retain the character of a rural English life that has largely disappeared in other parts of the country.

We should thank the Waveney that this is so. The river forms marshland that has always been awkward to cross. No great high roads pass from the south to Norwich via either Beccles or Bungay. There is no coast road in Suffolk. The main trunk-road in the Waveney Valley, the A143, is on the northern, Norfolk side of the river and bypasses both towns. As a result, the country to the south of Bungay is rural, quiet and isolated, even to this day. Although it is only 120 miles from London this wide area of small and scattered villages is relatively undisturbed by traffic. It is an ideal terrain for cycling, whether practised as a pastime or as a sport.

Here, in February of 1953, the Godric Cycling Club was born. George King was not originally a Suffolk man. He was an Essex boy from Romford, and a member of the Becontree Wheelers before World War II. After the war he lived and worked in Surrey and joined the newly formed Surrey Ravens C.C., based in Caterham. He then moved to London and worked for Holdsworth, but still rode with the 'Ravens'. He met Daphne Coles at a Kent Cycling Association dinner in 1950, where he had gone to collect his silver medal for First Handicap prize in the K.C.A. 100 of that year.

Daphne was not a club cyclist but, since her early teens, had ridden tandem and solo with her father – a prominent figure in the Kent C.A. – before he moved to the Essex/Suffolk border. The Coles Trophy, which is awarded to the winner of the Godric's championship 50, is named in his honour. George and Daphne cycled with the Surrey Ravens C.C. until they moved to Bungay in October 1952.

1

In 1953, therefore, we already find a characteristic of the Godric C. C. Its roots are in its native country, but the club's membership has always been replenished by cyclists who have come to north Suffolk from other parts of Britain, primarily the south-east. These newcomers are generally in the later years of life. But the Godric C.C. emphasises youth. The club's most enthusiastic members have almost always been young people who were born and bred in the region. Most of the people who joined George and Daphne King were teenagers, but they immediately became officers of the new organisation.

The founding date was 13 February 1953. About 30 people attended an inaugural meeting at the Market Tea Rooms in Bungay. The general desire to form the club was obvious, and the procedural difficulties were skilfully managed by George King. Bungay's cycling club then began with eighteen members, among whom we note the names of Geoff Mayne, Maurice Riches and Peter Roe.

What would be the name of the club? Some local connection was desirable. In the 1930s there had been a Bigod C.C., named after the Earls of Bungay Castle, but nobody wished to revive the name of a defunct club. George King had the answer. Godric was the original owner of the land on which Bungay and its castle were built. So the name of the Godric C.C. (which has puzzled many people) refers to a period before the Norman Conquest.

No other British cycling club announces that its name has a connection with Saxon times. Yet the young Godric C.C. did not have an antiquarian spirit. It joined a golden age of the sport. Thoughts were of the future. By the year of the Queen's coronation post-war austerity had relaxed. Mass motoring had not begun. The British cycle trade was successful as never before nor since. There was a new feeling of social progress. Many people who had returned from the war wished to explore their native land. Often they did so by bicycle, and with their young families. So it is not surprising that, in the early 50s, new clubs were formed all over the country. The Godric C.C. was part of a much wider movement.

The club immediately became part of a local fellowship. There were friendly relations – soon there would be cheerful racing rivalries – with the Lowestoft Wheelers, the Diss and District C.C., the East Anglian C.C. and the Norwich A.B.C. A number of the teenage Godrics were riding to their first jobs and apprenticeships in Norwich, so it was natural that their club should affiliate to the Norwich Cycling Association.

The club also affiliated to the National Cyclists' Union and the Road Time-Trials Council. As a member of these organisations the Godric C.C.

was ready for a racing programme. First of all came the club-runs. These shared Sunday-morning expeditions left from the Old Butter Cross, the heart of Bungay. They occupied a full day. Lunch was carried, and there were halts for elevenses and at favoured tea places. The runs visited such places as Framlingham, Bury St Edmunds, Surlingham Ferry and Walsham le Willows. The usual distance for one of these days was 70–80 miles.

The runs were planned, and afterwards discussed, at midweek meetings. At first the Market Tea Rooms was the headquarters. Then a new clubroom was found. It was in the White Lion Inn (where Godrics practised the skills that for many years would make them darts champions within the Norwich C.A.). But much of the talk was of competition. The club's colours had been decided and the road jerseys were ordered. The green, yellow and red were taken from the escutcheon of the Earls of Bigod. Training began in earnest, and soon the young Godrics were ready for the unique excitement of cycle-racing.

The first Godric C.C. race was a ten-mile time-trial. It was held on the old stretch of Roman Road toward Halesworth known as 'the Bungay straight'. History demands that the course should be recorded, and in the official language of the RTTC:

START approx. 120 yards south of Ilketshall Hall entrance TURN at electric pole No.DP 81 near entrance to Grain Factory RETRACE past start to Finish approx. 400 yds south of St John's Church.

Seven riders were in contention. The winner was Peter Roe, the only young man among them with previous racing experience. This historic 10 was soon followed by a 25. The older Godrics had measured a Waveney Valley course between Flixton and Billingford. The weather might have been devised by the demonic Black Dog that haunts the church and people of Bungay. Only three riders started in the high winds and cold, pouring rain. Barry Minns was the first home. His time of 1.13.38 indicated the conditions in which he and two other pioneers had to compete.

Next, a 50. The course was an extension of the 25. The small field sped through Billingford to Scole and on to the main Norwich–Ipswich road, retracing after a far turn at Little Stonham. Barry Minns returned to the timekeeper with a 2.25.8, an excellent performance from a 16 year old in his first season. He was followed by Barry Holmes, Peter Roe and Ken Whiteland. Geoff Mayne, who was a marshal, recalls gathering mushrooms in meadowland near Flixton. Then there was a celebratory breakfast, cooked on a primus stove, after they clapped the finishers.

In this way Barry Minns became the first Godric to win the Coles Trophy. From that day to our own the 50 championship has had an especial status within the club, fittingly commemorated in the jubilee year of 2003 with the Godric's promotion of the National Championship 50. Half a century ago the youthful champion Barry Minns led the Godric team to their first appearance in an open event. It was the Norwich A.B.C. 100. The other young men who carried the Godric colours in this demanding test were Peter Roe, Maurice Riches and Ken Whiteland.

It is a tradition of cycling that the time-trialling season ends with a hill-climb. There are no long hills in the Bungay area, but a number of short, deceptive and awkward ascents. In 1953 the first of several hill-climb courses used by the Godrics was Dove Hill at Homersfield, sometimes known in the neighbourhood as Holbrook Hill at Alburgh. The short stretch of road soon becomes 1 in 9, then rears to 1 in 6 before 100 yards of *faux-plat* before the finish. The surface is sandy and slippery. As would be proved many times in years to come, Dove Hill is suited to a grass-track man with a powerful sprint. In 1953 Peter Roe went up in 40 seconds.

Daphne King
by George King

George King
by Daphne King

4

CHAPTER 2

After the hill-climb, mince pies and the beginning of the social season.
The Godric year ended with a dinner and prize presentation at the Three
Tuns Hotel. It is interesting to look at the menu that was printed for this
occasion. The Godric membership was young, high-spirited and often re-
bellious. Yet the club followed the dignities of much older organisations.
A three-course meal was served by waiters. The men wore suits and their
wives or girlfriends wore gowns. There was a loyal toast to the Queen.
Speeches accompanied further toasts to 'The Club', then 'The Ladies',
'The Visitors and Press', and finally 'The Prize-winners'.

At this first dinner George and Daphne King must have looked with
pleasure at the society they had created. Its achievement was impressive.
The infant club had come to maturity in fewer than twelve months. On the
other hand, it was still a small group of friends. At the end of 1953 the total
membership was around 20 and there were not more than seven or eight
racing members. In the later 1950s there would not be much change in the
essential nature of the Godric. The founding members continued to be the
major prize-winners. There was a mixture of lively competitiveness and a
growing sense among the teenagers that cycling was not merely a hobby,
but a way of life. So the main task of the club was to build and consolidate.

Some local and individual factors helped the club as it grew. First of
all, some notable and inspiring friends joined the Godric. These new members were sometimes experienced cyclists who favoured the Godric over
their previous clubs. Prominent among such new recruits was Cyril Wigby.
Another reason for the growth of the club is paradoxical. The Godric C.C.
developed from a sapling to a sturdy young tree not only because of enthusiasm but also because of the conservative nature of the country in which
it thrived.

In this part of East Anglia social change was slow to come, in part
because of its remoteness (remote from London, that is) and partly because of its dependence on agriculture. Wages were low, for anyone in the
rural economy. In the cities, young people were beginning to buy motor-
cycles and cars. This trend was hardly apparent in the Waveney Valley.
Even with the expansion of printing works at Beccles and Bungay most
people naturally went to work by bicycle; and so it was also natural to use
the bike for pleasure, for the exploration of a countryside where railways
and bus routes did not exist.

The bicycle was also used for sport. The agricultural background helps
to explain the survival of grass-track racing in East Anglia. In the mid

An Attleborough Whit Monday Sports Day: Barry Minns is on the extreme left

Massed-start "Rough Stuff", 1954. (left to right) Geoff Mayne, John Pugh,
Barry Minns, Sam Patrick, Ken Whiteland, Daphne King

6

1950s the nearest made-up track to Bungay was the asphalt oval at Kettering, many miles distant. But grass tracks can be devised wherever there is level grass (or nearly level, in many cases) and the racing was always good-humoured. It was easy to enter on the line, there was a trackside audience, the afternoon was shared with athletic and other events, and the atmosphere had the jollity of a rural sports day. So we find that Godrics competed in such events as the Norwich A.B.C. and East Anglia R.C. Championships, held on a playing field at Attleborough; and they were also at meetings at Brantham, Eye and Harleston; and joined the races that celebrated the Laxfield and District Horticultural and Poultry Society's Annual Show.

The Godric's new member Cyril Wigby was an expert in this branch of cycle sport. He had first raced on grass in the 1930s. Cyril and his wife Edna were to give much to the Godric in the years to come. The Edna Wigby Memorial Rose Bowl, subscribed for by members and friends in 1969, is awarded each year to a member who has done most to promote the well-being of the club.

Off-road cycling is a Godric tradition. Grass-track competition has never entirely disappeared and in 1955 the club began 'rough stuff' racing, as it was then called. 'Mud plugging' would soon become the more sophisticated sport of cyclo-cross. The first Godric event of this sort was held in 1955 on a five-mile course around Ditchingham. Among the entries we find the names of lads who would be prominent in the annals of the club: Geoff Mayne, Barry Minns, Sam Patrick, John Pugh and Ken Whiteland. And, looking forward only three years, to 1958, we find the name of the teenager Lindsay Wigby, who rode strongly in his first off-road race. Cyril and Edna's son was not only a competitor. For many years he has organised cyclo-cross events, especially on Broome Heath, to the great delight of all Godrics and many visiting crossmen.

x   x   x   x   x

Veterans of 1950s Waveney valley cycling look back on optimistic days while also mentioning that there were at least two threats to the future of the Bungay club. The first (say these veterans, often in jest) was marriage. The second was National Service. Young men found that they had a relish for cycling life. Then they were sent from their homes to spend two years in futile military exercises. Here was a nationwide problem for cycling clubs, for National Servicemen often did not take their bikes out of the shed once they had taken off uniform and returned to civilian work.

However, almost all the teenagers who were founder members of the Godric did their National Service and also came back to cycle sport. Some of them also returned to marriage. The responsibilities of finding a new home and building a family did not keep them from cycling. We may also be sure that many a union was helped by that old instrument of courtship, the tandem.

Godric marriages run through the history of the club. The Godric was never an all-male society (as some cycling clubs still were, at least until the end of the 60s), and of course its members were likely to marry each other. In a newspaper cutting of about 1960 we find the cynical comment that the Godric C.C. was 'like a marriage bureau'. This was quite mistaken. Marriage bureaux help people who are lonely and unhappy. The members of Bungay's cycling club were not at all lonely. They were healthy, optimistic and took pleasure in company. By 1961 there had already been five Godric marriages. There were to be many more cyclists' weddings. Godric marriages produced Godric children and now, in 2003, there are also Godric grandchildren. One day we must organise a party for them.

x   x   x   x   x

Among the first of the Godric married couples were Roland and Doreen Stevenson. Roly had become a cyclist in 1948. After completing National Service he joined the club in 1955. With Roly came his young wife, whom he had already introduced to the fellowship of the wheel.

In the later 1950s Roly Stevenson combined his racing career with a number of other roles. He was Runs Captain, the editor of the Godric Newsletter and the leader of many expeditions to youth hostels. Younger Godrics had already become YHA members and enjoyed weekends in more simple conditions than are offered to the hostellers of today. Among their favourite resting places were the hostels at Blaxham, near Ipswich, and Sheringham on the north-Norfolk coast. Some of these young people had never left East Anglia. With Roly Stevenson as their leader they went on Godric tours, generally over the Easter holiday, to Wales or Yorkshire. It is said that Roly often had to explain to youth-hostel wardens that his younger clubmates were not misbehaved, simply high-spirited …

Doreen Stevenson, over the years, must have met more racing Godrics on more occasions than any other club official, and also met their racing rivals, for she has been the timekeeper since 1972:

And our sparkling eyed timekeeper
Sparkling eyes for ever watching
Watching seconds slowly creeping
Creeping slowly round the dial …

As a Godric poet, inspired by Longfellow's *Hiawatha*, once remembered her.

Today's fast men will be glad to recall that the much-loved Doreen Stevenson was the Godric's leading woman time triallist in the early 1960s. She was Club Secretary from 1964 to 1976, and Events Secretary from 1976 to 1993. Most of these Godric events were time-trials. By its nature, time-trialling requires more bureaucracy than other sports. The task of filling in forms with individual times requires long hours of work from a selfless worker who helps other people to enjoy bike-racing. Any kind of road-racing also depends on friendly dealings with the police. Doreen Stevenson, with other club officials, established good relations with the local force. Members of the local police force are often guests at Godric dinners and there have been Godric members with professional careers as policemen.

At the first club dinner, 1953

9

NORFOLK NEWS, FRIDAY, DECEMBER 17, 1954

By Bike To Church

CYCLISTS from many parts of Norfolk attended the carol service at Pulham St. Mary on Sunday, organised by the Norwich Cycling Association. Here the Rev. C. G. Kerslake is seen showing some of his congregation features of the church before the service began, and, in the other picture, giving the address during the service.

The Cyclists' Carol Service, Pulham St Mary, 1954

CHAPTER 3

In the later 1950s, when the Godrics welcomed the interest of the Wigbys and the Stevensons, the club's racing members were also cycle tourists, and all members enjoyed activities that were not related to the bicycle. The fast men, the ladies and the tourists were together when they rode to the cyclists' carol service at Pulham St Mary (first attended by the Godrics in 1954, beginning a tradition that has lasted to this day); and they were together when they held running races on the beach at Covehithe, or when they played darts, or joined the scavenger hunts, map-reading contests, tourist quizzes, and freewheeling competitions.

These diversions were sometimes judged on a points system. They lasted well into the 60s and in 1965 the Gong Trophy was inaugurated and given to a person who had done well in the 'special events'. In 1954 the various contests helped to maintain the communal Godric spirit. The weather that summer was so bad that the racing season had little meaning. Many a darts match was played while the Godrics waited eagerly for spring and new challenges.

The great innovation of 1955 was the Godric C.C.'s entry to massed-start racing. It began with a triumph. Geoff Mayne battled around a 48-mile course to become the Eastern Counties Cycling Association's junior champion. The club had no entry in the senior event for the simple reason that all its racing members were juniors. But the future would be theirs!

In June of 1955 the Godric C.C. unanimously decided to affiliate to the British League of Racing Cyclists. In other parts of Britain there would have been many clubroom arguments about such a step. In East Anglia, however, there were fewer differences between the adherents of the BLRC and the NCU. So the way forward was clear. In August the Godric pioneers Geoff Mayne, Barry Minns and John Pugh went south to Ipswich to contest another Eastern Counties Championship. Mayne, Minns and Pugh also raced in massed-start events on the Ellough airfield course and took part in the Tour of the East Coast, with a finish at Pakefield.

Time-trialing was not ignored and it was mostly the same riders who competed, week after week, in the club 10s, 25s and the 50, while going further afield to enter other 50s or 100s. They were all-rounders. In November the same keen riders – Minns, Mayne, Patrick and Pugh – took part in their first roller contest, held at St Giles Hall in Norwich.

At the end of the 1955 season Barry Minns again became the club champion. He was a worthy victor and a rider who set a standard for all his clubmates. The Godric championships were based on the conventional

11

time-trial distances. There was also an interest in solo against-the-clock trials over distances between Bungay and other towns. They were always Bungay-and-back, as in the usual routine of the time-trial.

These 'place-to-place' or 'point-to-point' record attempts were undertaken by only one rider, who therefore had a solitary experience. There was no-one to catch up with the competitor, no minute-man in sight. On quiet and mostly empty roads, early on Sunday morning, when mist lifted to warm sunshine, no one was about – except fellow Godrics who had gathered at the turn or a roundabout to shout encouragement and hand up sponges or bottles. Rides of great beauty were achieved, though the cyclist making the record attempt was probably suffering too much to notice, and the only audience was a handful of clubfolk, and perhaps a few early church-goers who had no idea what was happening.

National place-to-place records in the 1950s, an important part of both amateur and professional cycling at that time, mainly followed the high roads from London to provincial capitals. Clubs such as the Godric devised routes to places that were nearer their home town, and the rides always returned to that town. It is now difficult for anyone to judge place-to-place records. They have become confused by road improvements and traffic conditions. The roads are faster, towns and former villages are congested. It therefore seems best to give a list of the Godric's place-to-place courses as they were in 1962, just before the sudden expansion of motor traffic and new building in East Anglian towns. For obvious reasons, some of these records are no longer disputed. The mileage is given as Bungay-and-back.

MEN:
Yarmouth 38; Aldburgh 50; Bury St Edmunds 72; Ipswich 74; Cromer 78; London (GPO, E12) 198.
WOMEN:
Beccles 11; Harleston 15; Halesworth 18; Lowestoft 30.

Readers will note that, in 1962, it was still possible to ride in and out of central London on a record attempt. In the 1950s some Godrics rode to London for other reasons, mostly to the Good Friday meeting at Herne Hill Stadium, where they would see national and international trackmen. Towards the end of the 1950s there was a tendency for the Godrics to ride longer distances. The teenagers who had been co-founders of the club were on their way to physical maturity. They were hoping to ride 100s and 12s. Therefore, the club-runs became longer and often were used as training rides. Here are the club-runs for the early summer of 1958. The town or villages named were halts for elevenses, lunch (almost always carried), and tea:

20.4.58 Scole, Bury St Edmunds, Long Stratton
27.4.58 Wymondham, Acle, Lowestoft
4.5.58   Attleborough, Ixworth, Harleston
11.5.58 Kelsale, Wickham Market, Thwaite
18.5.58 Wymondham, Guist, Beccles
25.5.58 Bury St Edmunds, Lavenham, Thwaite
1.6.58   Wymondham, Aylsham, Great Yarmouth
8.6.58   Wymondham, Thetford, Harleston
15.6.58 Wymondham, Stalham, Lowestoft
22.6.58 Wymondham, Mundesley-on-Sea, Great Yarmouth
29.6.58 Wroxham, Cromer, Norwich

Wymondham was a popular place for a midsummer elevenses because it was on the fast time-trialing course used by the Norwich clubs. Godrics went there to support their clubmates in a time-trial or simply to look at their future opposition. At Wymondham, after their events, Godric racing members joined their touring friends. As we can see, they then took the long way home. They probably rode around 100 miles before returning to Bungay on Sunday evenings. If they were also doing 30–40 a day as work miles – since so many of them had jobs in Norwich – and were sharpening their speed in evening 10s, as well as doing other types of training, then it is likely that they were entering 300–400 miles a week in their diaries and mileage charts.

These numerous hard miles had an immediate benefit. A handful of Godrics were soon able to challenge for high honours in the very longest of cycle races. In 1956 John Pugh entered his first 24, the North Road C.C. promotion. He was only nineteen years old. Thus began a long-distance career that is without equal, and of which we will hear much more. But there was a disadvantage to the fast club-run miles. There was a growing division between the racing members and their comrades who rode only for pleasure, and at a moderate pace.

It was not a social division, just a selection on the road. The same thing happens in most cycling clubs. It was fortunate that all the members were soon able to gather together in a new headquarters. In February of 1958 the Godric C.C. celebrated its fifth birthday by moving into its own clubroom. It was not a splendid building. The Godric made their home in one of the former prisoner-of-war huts on Hillside Road. But it was a special place for every member. Club nights were held on Wednesday evenings. Godrics played darts and table tennis. They exchanged views on cycling and life, in that order. There was a set of rollers and facilities for making tea.

John Pugh starts in the North Roads C.C. 24, 1956

At the new clubroom, 1958

CHAPTER 4

Surviving photographs of the club taken in 1957–8 show that a number of members' bikes were carrying spare wheels tied to the handlebars with toe-straps. This is a sure sign that the 'spares' were actually sprint wheels that had been used for racing earlier in the day. The photographs do not reveal much more detail about the bicycles, not even their make. In rural East Anglia there was no strong tradition of local frame builders. From anecdotal evidence it seems likely that most racing men in the Godric favoured Holdsworth, Ephgrave or Carlton frames. Not everyone had derailleur gears, perhaps because they were costly. Riding on a fixed wheel probably survived for longer in Suffolk than in other parts of the country. The Godrics often bought their equipment from the specialist shop in Diss run by Eric Madgett. He was a friend of the club, as he was of all clubs. Mr Madgett was a great patron of cycle sport throughout East Anglia. He was guest of honour at the 1959 dinner. By chance, one of the remarks in his speech was prophetic of a future phase in the development of the Godric club. He entered a plea for cycling to be a sport in all schools. In other parts of Mr Madgett's address he spoke of the achievements of the club, its prize-winners, and its place in Suffolk and Norfolk cycling. We can now look at some of these achievements in 1958 and 1959.

First, a bureaucratic and geographical note. The club's racing programme, if it was not to be the same dozen Godric riding against each other week after week, depended on cycling associations, their promotions, records, their encouragement of open events and BAR competitions. The Norwich Cycling Association (founded in 1939) was important to the Godric because it provided a variety of races and had a growing number of member clubs.

In the late 50s the clubs who were eligible to affiliate to the N.C.A. were those within a 30 mile radius of Norwich. In 1964 this radius was enlarged to 50 miles. The Godrics' racing activities tended to enlarge in the same way and within the same area. Even when the fast men (especially in the 1970s) were tempted to dragstrip courses towards the London end of the A12 there was not much desire to compete against the clubs in London, the Midlands or further afield. This is still the case. Few East Anglian riders from the old N.C.A. clubs contest the National Best All-Rounder Championship.

Early in 1958 the Godrics challenged more established clubs at the Attleborough meeting of the NCU Eastern Counties Centre. In the two-mile pursuit the team from Bungay was Pete Gilding, Geoff Mayne, Barry

Minns and Sam Patrick. They swept to victory on a wet, slow track. In midsummer there was a camping weekend near the source of the Waveney and then, in September, a visit to Herne Hill stadium for the famous 'Coppi meeting', where a huge crowd gathered to see the legendary Fausto, a link with the greatest days of European cycle-racing.

Team Pursuit Champions, East Anglia Division:
(left to right) Pete Gilding, Sam Patrick, Geoff Mayne, Barry Minns

As sometimes happens, the best ride of the season was accomplished in the golden weather of a Michaelmas summer. On 12 October Barry Minns contested the Norwich A.B.C. 25 and beat the hour for the first time in his short and radiant career. He recorded 58.30 and thus became one of only six Suffolk riders to break through the 60-minute barrier. The sequence of club evening 10s on the Halesworth road came to its close with notes for the future, in the form of a fine win by Dave Hatcher and a promising beginning by young Lindsay Wigby.

At the end of the year the Godric C.C. had the following tally of successes. The racing members had made themselves prominent throughout the region. Eight of them had competed on the road in 27 open events and had taken 31 prizes, including five firsts, five seconds, five thirds, four fourths and seven handicap prizes. In addition, the club's finances were sound and there were 41 members, most of them active. If they were not racing or touring in club-runs they gave help as timekeepers and marshals.

Secretarial help was also needed as the Godric planned its first open road-race. On a rainy December morning a small group took to the fields to get past floods between Homersfield and Mendham, then rode to Metfield and Halesworth before returning to Bungay. Familiar territory, but planning was essential before police co-operation was granted, and the club's organising committees sent out invitations and entry forms. How would a large group of racing cyclists negotiate the lanes and corners that the Godrics knew so well but might be quite new to other competitors?

It was difficult to devise a course south of Bungay that wasn't intricate. When the event took place in April of 1959 some riders criticised a route that took 40 starters over 64 miles on a course that started outside the clubroom, then linked Bungay with Homersfield, Mendham, Rumburgh and St Lawrence. But the race was a success, with a crowd at the finish. There were teams from 10 East Anglian clubs and a prestigious winner, Bill Seggar (Suffolk Roads C.C.) who that year was the national road-race champion. Barry Minns, Seggar's main rival in this and many other events, was in second place.

*Start of the first road-race promoted
by Godric C.C., April 1959*

17

This event was followed by a far more important road-race. The three-day Tour of East Anglia was held over Whitsun. It went from Ipswich to Norwich, Norwich to Cambridge and Cambridge to Ipswich. The total distance was 335 miles. The Godric team consisted of now familiar racing men: Mayne, Minns, Patrick and Pugh. They were riding against professionals, independents and at least one former Olympic roadman. In a way, this Tour was a contest between riders from the N.C.A. clubs and more prominent roadmen from all over the country. Geoff Mayne and Barry Minns joined Ipswich-based Bill Seggar as the best-placed locals.

Bill Seggar enters a history of the Godric C.C. because he lived in East Anglia, was of national and indeed international class and therefore gave an especial edge to the provincial cycle sport. The young Godrics could see that they were not far removed from national standards. Seggar won the East Anglian Road Race Championship in June of 1959. Minns and Mayne came second and third. Sixth-placed rider Sam Patrick secured the team prize for the Godric C.C.

x   x   x   x   x

Turning now to time-trialing at the end of the 1950s, we see that the Godrics were powerful both in open competition and their own club events. Consider, for instance, a pioneering team time trial promoted by the Norwich A.B.C., and then the struggle for the Godric Best All-Rounder trophy.

The Norwich A.B.C. event had a full card. It was contested over 38 miles by 23 three-up teams. At the end of the morning the Godric 'A' team was victorious. It consisted of Geoff Mayne, Barry Minns and Pete Gilding. There was also a Godric 'B' team in the race, made up of Dave Hatcher, Sam Patrick, and John Pugh. They took fourth place. The Godrics therefore placed no fewer than six riders among the dozen best East Anglian time-trialists. It is interesting to note that Godric 'A' all rode 84-inch fixed wheels on a blustery morning when many people preferred variable gears. The Best All-Rounder trophy was purchased from the club funds in 1959 and at the end of the season was awarded to Roly Stevenson. Now we can look at the way he defended his title in 1960.

Stevenson began his campaign in the Glade C.C. promotion on an Essex course. Then he was the fastest Godric in the Essex and Suffolk 100. Behind him, but not by far, were Pete Gilding and John Pugh. Then Pugh challenged Stevenson in the Norwich A.B.C. 50 and was on equal terms with the older rider after the Norwich C.A. 100. Stevenson replied with his fastest ever 50 in the West Suffolk Wheelers event. Not far behind was Dave

18

Hatcher, who looked good in the club 50 (won by Barry Minns) and then rode an excellent 12 in Essex, beating both Pugh and Stevenson. Next, Stevenson took five minutes from Pugh in the Colchester 50. Finally, Pugh decided to reply in the Oldbury 12 while Stevenson elected to ride the Eagle R.C. 50.

In this way Stevenson became the Godric BAR for a second year. The manner of his victory tells us that the competition among the top Godric riders was ever more keen, and also that they selected their races with care and travelled beyond the East Anglian region – but not very far beyond – in search of fast times.

This would be a pattern in the new decade. In other ways the Godric club remained its old self, with a mixed programme of club-runs, grass-track racing, evening 10s on the Halesworth road and recreations in the clubroom. Roly Stevenson and John Pugh attacked place-to-place records between Bungay and Cromer, and Bungay and Bury St Edmunds; and Pugh joined the camping section at Syleham after his Bury ride. Someone had caught a pike. It was cooked over a wood fire and shared by all before a night under canvas, not far from the silently moving Waveney, the stars and the moon above.

Camping at Syleham, 1960

Brian Harper (left) wins another grass event

CHAPTER 5

The campers at Syleham (where the Godrics knew a friendly landowner) were the nucleus of a successful and an expanding club. They looked toward victories and records. There is one obvious reason why these young people, as the 1960–61 social season ended, thought more about racing than about touring. They were strong and extremely fit. The teenagers who were among the club's founding members were now, seven years on, in their early twenties. They had arrived at the age of the first physical maturity of a bike rider.

At the end of the 50s the first Godric generation, led by Geoff Mayne, Barry Minns and John Pugh (all of whom had lost part of their cycling lives because of National Service) were joined by others who were perhaps three or four years younger. Among them were Richard Edwards, Pete Gilding, Dave Hatcher, Mick Harrison, Richard Pulford and Peter Roe. A prominent older rider was of course Roly Stevenson, and in 1962 the club welcomed Jimmy Smith, a racing man who had been in the bike game before the Godric was founded. Another slightly older rider was Brian Harper, a prolific winner of grass and cyclo-cross events.

No one in this élite group was complacent, but they were all enlivened by the arrival of a dazzling newcomer. He was Adrian Perkin, who joined the club in 1960, at the age of seventeen. In the following year he won the club 50, among other triumphs, and a brave ride in the Luton Wheelers 12 made him the Godric BAR in his first competitive season.

Adrian Perkin was a mile-eater and a keen youth-hosteller who rode all over England before returning to Bungay to test the legs of the local champions. He was also a dedicated tricyclist, as were a number of other members of the club. At one period in the early 60s we find that no fewer than six Godrics were riding the same events on trikes. In winter, the machine was often preferred for training and general riding on muddy or icy roads. Needless to say, the fastest time trials were ridden on two wheels. In Perkin's earlier career his best performance was also a test of stamina, a 241 in the National Championship 12. In this race he was well supported by John Pugh and Roy Pulford.

In 1962 and 1963 Perkin was the N.C.A. Best All-Rounder. At the end of 1962 he and some clubmates rode to London for the RTTC Champions' Night, held in those days at the Albert Hall. The Godric long-distance riders must have thought that they would be contenders for the team prize in the next year's half-day events. It was not to be, partly because potential members of a winning Godric team, especially Geoff Mayne and Barry

21

Minns, had loosened their commitment to racing. Both had new duties as young fathers.

The Guest of Honour at the tenth annual dinner (held at the King's Head in Bungay) was George Stockdale, who lived in Beccles. Mr Stockdale had been a top-class time-trialist before Hitler's war. In those days he rode with the Century R.C. and the Verulam C.C. Mr Stockdale's speech observed that the racing scene was more lively than it had been in his youth. His interest in the club was much appreciated and in 1963 he was formally invited to become the first President of the Godric C.C.

Mr Stockdale had much to observe in the 1963 season. Adrian Perkin continued his winning ways. John Bunyard, another newcomer of exceptional promise, became the club 50 champion while beating Barry Minns' record for the distance. Perkin set a new 25-mile trike record and recorded 243 miles in the National Championship 12 on a Lancashire course. John Pugh did 402 miles in the National 24 Championship. Meanwhile, two recruits to the club, April Moyse (later Roe) and Heather White announced a new era of women's racing in the Godric colours.

It was a time of vital and varied competition. Every month of the 1964 season brought some new racing adventure. In March four Godric teams raced in the Norwich A.B.C. two-up 25. At Easter a group of Godric hard men went for a training ride – to Sheffield, returning via Coventry, thus putting 450 miles in the bank. Geoff Mayne recorded a 1.0.35 to win the West Suffolk Wheelers 25, with the Godric taking the team prize. Then Mayne slashed over a minute from the Godric 25 course record with a 1.0.50 and the following Sunday raced to a 1.59.55 second place in the West Suffolk Wheelers 50. A fortnight later he took eight minutes from his personal best in the Norwich A.B.C. 100.

Distances lengthened as the season went on. All three Godrics in the East Midlands C.C. 12 recorded personal bests. Mayne rode 252 miles, Perkin 247 and Pugh 238. The three claimed second place in the team prize. Next, Mayne became the 25 Champion of the BCF East Anglia Division with a 58.47 and also won the club's 50 championship. For the first time the Godric C.C. entered a team in a 24. John Pugh, the acknowledged leader in distance racing, was forced to retire: but Mayne finished with 421 miles and Adrian Perkin with 387. John Bunyard, who had enjoyed himself in mass-start racing for most of the season, took the Aldeburgh-and-back record and at the end of the year Brian Harper won the hill-climb.

There was much more racing of this sort, as there was to be in 1965. And, as all racing men know, the quest for fast times can become obsessive.

The top riders were making the club glorious but the club as a whole began to show signs of weakness and strain. In January of 1965 the club membership had declined to 37. That month the guest speaker at the club dinner was Eric Moody of the Edgware R.C. He said that the Godric had the potential to become one of the top clubs in the country but begged the members 'not to let the social side go'. It was a timely word of warning. Mr Moody spoke as he did because he came from a London club. It was the mid-60s, a time of devastating change in social and recreational habits, especially among the young. In London these changes had already affected the cycling world. The 'social side' of life among wheelfolk was about to disappear.

In the Waveney Valley, as usual, there was less hurry to change old ways. Although the Godric C.C. was dominated by its racing members there was still a social and touring programme. Here, for instance, is the runs-list for the late autumn and winter of 1965:

Oct. 1-3	Camping in Thetford Forest
Oct. 10	Westleton Walks
Oct. 16–17	YHA weekend Sheringham, run to Blakeney Point
Oct. 24	Impromptu ride after the club 25
Oct. 31	Ride to the N.C.A. hill climb at Ringland
Nov. 6–7	Thetford youth hostel
Nov. 14	Free-wheeling contest
Nov. 21	Primus dinner at Westleton Walks
Nov. 28	Speed-judging contest
Dec. 3–5	Ride through Friday night to London for Holland Park youth hostel then Albert Hall, ride home, Sunday dinner Cozy café
Dec. 11–12	Blaxhall youth hostel then all to carol service, Pulham St Mary
Dec. 19	Christmas party, Sheringham youth hostel
Dec. 25	East Anglian C.C. 10
Dec. 31	Night ride to see the New Year in with Lowestoft Wheelers

Most of these activities, once so common, had already been abandoned by the racing cycling clubs of the 1960s. The Godric continued with such innocent country pleasures for some time. Veterans of the world of cycling will note that the above runs-list resembles the programme of any local branch of the Cyclists Touring Club of the 1950s. This brings us to the question of the Godric C.C.'s independence, its mixture of old and new. The CTC was never particularly active in north Suffolk or Norfolk. Indeed, the Norwich Cycling Association had been set up – back in 1939 – partly because of a feeling that the CTC was essentially a London organisation (which was not true) and that the CTC would give no help to racing cyclists (which was partly true).

Many racing clubs founded at the same time as the Godric – often called 'road clubs' – were offshoots of the CTC District Association. Not so with the Godric C.C. Its immediate parents were George and Daphne King who, in 1964, were elected the first life members of the club; and from the first Godric days its parent organisation had been the Norwich Cycling Association. The N.C.A. was at heart a league for racing clubs, though it also campaigned for road safety. Touring cyclists, the NCA felt, should be left to do whatever they wished.

In 1965-6 there was no dispute in the Godric club between touring traditionalists and committed racing members, nor between old and young. As was said at the 1966 Annual General Meeting, 'Though a young club, we've got "instant tradition".' Yet there was a feeling of unease, especially within the club's committee. Its officers felt that they did the work and had provided the framework for both racing and social rides. Was their work taken for granted by the wider, though diminishing, membership? Perhaps. At all events, only one member apart from the club officials attended the 1965 Annual General Meeting.

In the next year the AGM was announced with a plea from the secretary, Doreen Stevenson, 'please turn up, if only to kick us out of our jobs'. Again the attendance was poor. The committee now issued a statement saying 'we are worried by the lack of people willing to help with committee work, clubroom, and clubroom attendance, and the general apathy which we feel exists among members ...' and soon afterwards the officers of the Godric C.C. decided to hold a Special General Meeting. The venue was The Triple Plea pub at Bedingham. All members and their families were begged to attend. There was to be only one item on the agenda: 'The Future of the Club'.

Club-run, late 1950s

Club members leave for the ride to The Triple Plea

April Roe at the start of a club 25, ahead of Jimmy Todd and Dave Hatcher, watched by Doreen Stevenson, Godric's timekeeper since 1972

Margaret Mayne starts a record attempt outside Bungay Post Office, pushed off by Lindsay Wigby; Cyril Wigby checks the watch

CHAPTER 6

As we know so well, the club did have a future, though its 'instant tradition' would change with the times. New generations ask for different things. Many of the people who rode to the Special General Meeting at the 'Trip' in Bedingham were the parents of young families. A photograph shows some of them with side-cars and child-back tandems. In this snapshot we may discern the young Kevin Mayne, who looks about two. Years later, in 1998, he was to become the Director of the Cyclists Touring Club. On his appointment Mayne junior emphasised that he came from a cycling family – by which, we may believe, he meant not only his own parents but the extended family of his north Suffolk club.

As if to emphasise that new times were arriving, the 1967 racing year began with promising rides by juniors and by women. Schoolboy Graham Todd impressed in the East Anglian C.C.'s 25 in April. So did another Godric junior, Ross Mullinger, with a plucky ride in his first open event. As spring turned to summer the Godric ladies were admired. Suzanne Trudgill and April Roe led the way in the early season followed by the experienced Doreen Stevenson and a newcomer to time-trialing, Margaret Mayne.

This was to be Margaret Mayne's season. She wore the Godric jersey in events throughout East Anglia and shared the honours with April Roe in the Godric's own events. Most notably, Mrs Mayne took the women's place-to-place records, all of which had previously been held by Doreen Stevenson. In June Adrian Perkin went under the hour for the first time, and in the next month all Godrics were on hand for the annual road-race, either as competitors or as marshals and officials.

This interesting two-stage (but one-day) road-race was part of the Beccles Festival of Sport but attracted riders from outside East Anglia, many of them first-category roadmen. In the morning there was a time-trial from Beccles to Bungay and back, going outward on the Suffolk side and returning on the northern side. In the afternoon there was a 40-mile massed-start race on Ellough airport, which meant 50 circuits of a tight, flat, and windswept course.

x   x   x   x   x

There were still worries about the future, perhaps the ethos, of the club. Roly Stevenson looked back to his own early racing days when he wrote in the Godric Newsletter:

Where is the friendly atmosphere we know existed a couple of decades ago? Clubmates would ride out to an event – perhaps twenty miles or more. Take part in the event and then pile into a café before a club-run through the lanes. The accent now is on the record, the time, the BAR placing … Why is it that the clubroom is uninhabited these nights? Television too interesting?

It is true that the clubroom was a problem. The old prisoner-of-war hut had been demolished and the Godrics were forced to hire a room in the Old Grammar School. The rent was far too high so the clubroom moved to the empty garage at 'Ourcave', Roly and Doreen Stevenson's home on Hillside Road.

In this garage the racing men talked about their training rides and their plans for the BAR championship. Since the club BAR included a 12 hour race all the racing members had an interest in this difficult event. They all wanted to prepare for a 12 with numerous fast miles. Club-runs were ignored and small chain-gangs made expeditions to turn at King's Lynn or Cambridge, carrying bonk bars and never lingering in cafés. And, since the best 100 and 12 courses were often at some distance from Bungay, a number of Godric members regularly went to a race by motor car.

The nearest 12 course to Bungay was that used by the West Suffolk Wheelers promotion. Its Breckland and Fenland roads are flat, even and monotonous – not necessarily the best combination for a lonely rider in a long event. The course is especially unpleasant in rain and wind. These were the conditions in 1969, when half the field of 60 retired. Godric Peter Roe stuck at his cold task and finished with 226 miles. This courageous ride ensured that he won the Godric BAR for the second year in succession. The Roe family were even happier when April won the ladies' BAR. Junior champion was Ross Mullinger.

Within a couple of seasons the talented Ross Mullinger would be riding on equal terms with the seniors and with such a veteran as Stan Foreman, who at the age of 42 came to the Godric from Barnet C.C. Stan Foreman was the first of the 'young veterans' who were to join the club in the next years, followed by Londoners who had also come to live in Bungay, Peter Bourchier (formerly West Kent R.C.) and Pat Sheppard (formerly Crest C.C.). An older cyclist than the new vets was Jimmy Todd. He had been a roadman in pre-war years and now rode against his son Graham Todd, who was Ross Mullinger's friend and rival.

Many racing cyclists are the sons – or, less often, the daughters – of other racing cyclists, and they ride out in each others' company. As the old cycling motto puts it, 'We're all young on the bike'. In our sport, racing careers can last for decades, and an interrupted career can be resumed after many years when a cyclist was 'out'. In this way there is a continuity between generations. Within the Godric C.C., however, the contrast between veteran and teenage cyclists became extreme. In the early 1970s the club recruited large numbers of schoolchildren. Their parents were rarely cyclists and generally knew little about the sport.

This initiative came from Geoff Mayne, a schoolteacher by profession. 'Mayne Gives other Cyclists a Lesson' was the headline in local newspapers after one of his many time trial victories. The history master was also dedicated to the idea that cycling should become a regular school sport. Only in quiet rural Suffolk could this idea be contemplated. Traffic conditions, and therefore parents' and headteachers' worries, soon overcame the project. For a while, however, Mayne was a leading figure in the English Schools Cycling Association. It did not flourish throughout the land, but E.S.C.A. did good work in some areas – especially in Bungay and Ipswich, where Mayne was a teacher.

Geoff Mayne in 1966

At the beginning of the 1970s a number of Godric club-runs coincided with runs under the *aegis* of the English Schools Cycling Association. As a result, some enthusiastic young people (mainly from Bungay Middle School) joined the club. Two of them were Frances Greenwood and Daphne Page, who were successful in the National Schools Cyclo-Cross Championships. Frances and Daphne were soon joined by Heather Patrick and then by three boys, Stephen Beckham, Paul Marshall, and Neil Patrick.

These schoolchildren responded well to difficult targets. There was a 100-mile reliability trial, for instance, the course for which was to be covered in six and a half hours. Among the young people who returned to Bungay within this time were Neil Patrick and Paul Marshall, both aged 12; Gordon Hazell, who was 14; and Heather Patrick and Daphne Page, both aged 15. Everyone was proud. But this sort of performance could be read in two ways. First, there were signs of racing promise in the young 100-milers. But, second, the reliability trial proved that a long cycle ride can be accomplished by any healthy young person.

One of the purposes of the E.S.C.A. was to show that this was so. Given the nature of the modern world, it was a utopian programme. The days of mass cycling were never to return. In the Waveney Valley, as elsewhere, cycling was becoming a slightly unusual pastime and a highly specialised sport. Despite changing times, the Godric still had a place at the heart of a rural community. Take, for instance, the club's appearance at the 1970 Beccles Festival of Sport.

Beccles may be an old-fashioned town; but it is not quaint and has many busy local societies. The Festival of Sport was organised by the Beccles Sports Development Council, whose new Sports Pavilion and Club, at Common Lane, was opened by the then Minister of Agriculture (the Rt. Hon. J. Prior) with varied music provided by the Beccles Salvation Army Band. There were athletic contests at this Festival of Sport, and the Godrics joined the runners in racing on grass, just as many of them had done in country sports days decades before.

The new Beccles Sports Centre had facilities used by local football, rugby, cricket and hockey clubs. The Council gave these societies interest-free loans for the purchase of equipment. In other words, local government looked kindly on sportspeople. The Godrics observed the situation of the Beccles sporting clubs with a slightly jealous interest, for they were still using the garage at 'Ourcave' as their clubroom.

It did not greatly matter. Cyclists are not restricted to a single field and a row of dismal pegs in a changing room. Their horizons are far away, on the adventure of the road. In 1970 Geoff Mayne ventured the furthest, for he took all six of the club's place-to-place records – including London-and-back, accomplished in nine and a half hours – and was the winner of the Luton Wheelers 12 with 249 miles.

Disappointment of the year was the Godric team's failure in the National Championships 100, held on a course that was familiar to them, the old B42 on the single-carriageway roads between Attleborough, Bury and Brandon. Cold, rainy weather spoiled the day. There were many punctures and retirements. So the Godrics could not match themselves against the cream of British cycling. And, to this day, we still ask whether Godric riders might have done better at national level, had their home roads not held their interest, and limited their ambitions.

There were plenty of opportunities to race within the locality. Dave Hatcher, for instance, who seldom travelled far to race, had ridden no fewer than 23 time-trials by August of the 1970 season. The clubs of the Norwich Cycling Association provided many opportunities for the fast men and there were often large fields. Evening 10s (which by this date were disappearing in the more built-up parts of the country) often had more than 50 riders. The Godric open 10 in May of 1971 attracted more than 100 entries, and this was by no means a prestigious event.

The new club room on Maltings Meadow

Kevin Norman

Club-run, January 1974

Because so many young people were members the Godric C.C. was well placed to appeal to the local Bungay council for help with the search for a clubroom. Club nights, after two long years in 'Ourcave' garage, were temporarily held in rooms belonging to the Lodge of Odd Fellows. Then the good news came that a hut on Maltings Meadow might be available for the club. Geoff Mayner was in charge of fund raising. Many other members helped with repairs and decoration. The club hut was formally opened in November of 1972. There were many celebrations, including a showing of the classic Tour de France film, *Pour un maillot jaune.*

The new clubroom would be the venue of many parties. The Godric also continued its annual dinners and prize-giving ceremonies. These ritualistic dinners, with their toasts, cross-toasting and speeches, have been an established part of cycling life, in clubs everywhere, since the 1890s. There were occasional suggestions within the Godric club that dinners should be replaced with a buffet supper or some other informal ceremony. However, tradition has always prevailed. Godric committees believe that decorum is a politeness extended to such guests as the Mayor of Beccles or the Town Reeve of Bungay.

Some changes could not be resisted. In 1972 the guest of honour at the annual dinner, held at the Sandringham Hotel in Great Yarmouth (because no more-local hostelry could accommodate the 120 guests) was Rex Coley. Mr Coley, then 74 years old, was a cyclist of the old school and was known as an opponent of music at club dinners. As 'Ragged Staff' he was still writing touring articles and gave lantern-slide lectures of an almost antique character. Prize-giving over, tables were cleared and the satanic noise of electric guitars filled the room. Mr Coley took to the floor and said to a girl 'I don't dance, but I'd like to hold you while you do!'

Happy days for young and old … At this dinner Alec Penman, in his first competitive year at the age of 30, was presented with the 1972 BAR trophy and said that he wished he had taken up cycling earlier in life. Adrian Perkin, now also aged 30, returned to cycling. In the first 25 of the season teenager Neil Skipper took first place in front of veteran Stan Foreman, who was racing before young Neil was born. 'Skip' went on to dominate the early season racing, won the 50 championship, rode a courageous West Suffolk Wheelers 12 and, although he was not old enough to be served in a pub, proposed the toast to 'The Guests' at the annual dinner.

Since the birth of the club, Godric officials had often been teenagers. In 1973 Neil Skipper was Events Secretary. Fifteen-year-old Kevin Norman, later to be the club's Chairman, was the Social Secretary, and the energetic young George Brown was the Clubroom Secretary. All these young officials were racing members. They were joined by people in their own age-group by, among others, John Dupen and Melvyn Phillips. In this year the veteran Roy Mobbs was a welcome new member, and all the more appreciated because he planned to open a specialist bike shop in Bungay.

x   x   x   x   x

Could anything be wrong with such a vital and growing club? One or two people feared that the Godric C.C. was out of control, and that its success was an illusion. It is true that a number of members with racing careers were seen no longer, and that many people joined the Godric but did not renew their membership twelve months later. One writer in the Godric newsletter was especially alarmed. He wrote that 'we have lost six of our most regular members and are shortly to lose more … a lot of our regular members turn up at the clubhouse less frequently …' and he also complained that the committee members were not doing a proper job.

The author of these criticisms was not a diplomat, and should have taken a longer view. The history of cycling clubs, wherever they have existed within the British Isles, tells us that there will be defections – maybe even a split – when a club's active members number more that about 60 to 70 people. That was the Godric C.C.'s position at the beginning of the 1970s. In this way it resembled other clubs. But there was a further complication. When the new clubroom opened in 1972 there were 74 members of the Godric, of whom 42 were schoolchildren. At the beginning of 1974 the membership was 67. Again, about half of these members were still at school.

To continue for a moment with the analysis of membership numbers: in February of 1974, the Godric's 21st birthday, no fewer than 238 cyclists had at different times been placed on the membership roll. The core members of the club were the officials, activists and racing champions who have already been mentioned in this book. By 1974 there had been perhaps two dozen of these dedicated Godrics. To their number we should add some family members who were also committed to the club but did not race or go to clubroom evenings. A young mother could not leave her house to play table tennis in a hut in Maltings Meadow, and why should she? But such a person was no less a Godric.

In any case, our rough statistics indicate that the Godric had a solid core, while there were any number of members who signed up, then came and went. The high number of 238 present and former members in 1974 would have included the intake of schoolchildren. They swelled the Godric's membership but were also least likely to remain in the club. The successive cohorts of children may have depressed older cyclists who did not wish to coach them or wait for them on club-runs. And, at this period, some members left the Godric for other reasons. They went to clubs that, superficially, had more glamour.

There is an independent assessment of the Godric C.C. at the beginning of 1974. It comes from Beryl Burton, who spoke at the club's dinner. Mrs Burton was not an intimate of the Godric. But the first lady of British cycling was a shrewd woman with a commitment to the club scene and must have attended many dozens of club dinners during her reign over the sport.

She could tell, almost instinctively, when a club was working well. That evening of the dinner, proposing a toast to the cyclists of Bungay, Mrs Burton said (according to the newspaper report) that the Godric C.C. seemed to 'have gone as far as it could in the field of schoolboy and schoolgirl cycling … But while 11-, 12-, 13- and 14-year-old cyclists were needed for the future of the sport a club also needed older riders and should have a string of cyclists from 11 years to 60 plus …'

Mrs Burton then congratulated the Godric C.C., wished its members health and happiness and said, 'Just keep those pedals turning, enjoy riding that bicycle and above all be proud that you are cyclists.'

These wise words are as relevant today as they were a quarter a century ago. Cycling is about happiness. Quarrels and disappointments in committees are alien to the spirit of the sport. All are agreed that young people should be encouraged to become cyclists. Yet there was something unbalanced, as Mrs Burton hinted, about a club with so many juniors and juveniles. Within a couple of years the balance was restored, with no harm done; and if we look at the riders who came to maturity in the Godric after childhood days in the English Schools Cycling Association then we can be sure that the club's interest in schoolchildren was beneficial.

x   x   x   x   x

A photograph of a club-run in January of 1974 shows sixteen Godrics (there were seventeen if we count the photographer), ten male, six female, perhaps eight of them of school age. It was a decent turn-out for a winter club-run, but might not have been typical. All too often there were only half a dozen cyclists at the Butter Cross meeting place on Sunday mornings.

In summer, other members would have been racing. Roly Stevenson, in the first 25 of the season, was challenged by the teenagers George Brown and Melvyn Philipps. In April all the Godrics applauded 12-year-old Wendy Page as she took the East Anglian Under-13 Schools Circuit Race Championship. Happy Wendy, in the new champion's jersey, had her picture in the newspaper. She was holding her Carlton bike, the saddle of which is right down on the top-tube.

Wendy and Daphne both rode well in the first 10 of the season. They were not the only young stars in this event. The terrific Kevin Norman (aged 15) relegated his coach, Geoff Mayne, to second place. The pupils were overtaking the schoolmasters, a development always to be welcomed. But young Kevin could not put Mr Mayne into detention. The history teacher won the East Anglian C.C. 50 and also the club 50 on the Earsham–Scole–Tasburgh course, then went south to take the first handicap in the Unity C.C. 25. In this year Mayne was BAR both of the Godric C.C. and the Norwich Cycling Association. And, unusually, he beat Lindsay Wigby in the hill-climb.

Wendy Page

36

CHAPTER 8

Lindsay Wigby, writing in the Godric newsletter in early 1975, lamented that 'the club-run is almost dead'. That spring a club-run list was still issued to members. The distances were shorter, down to about 50 miles. Destinations included Walberswick, Fressingfield and Woodbridge. In the racing season of 1975 the Godrics were offered the following menu:

Club Events
25 (late March)
25 (mid May)
50 (late June)
25 (early October)
Hill-climb (late October)
Together with 10s on Tuesday evenings at fortnightly intervals from late April.
Open Events
10 (on a mid-August Saturday) and a 25 on the following morning.
Cyclo-cross, Broome Heath (early December)
Track
Diss (late May)
Beccles SDC (mid June)
Diss (mid June)
Mildenhall (late August)
Together with racing every Wednesday evening, beginning in May, in the Norwich Cycling Association Track League.

Note that opportunities for massed-start racing are not even mentioned. But if we look at the programme that year of the BCF East Anglian Division we find road-races nearly every summer weekend. They were based on such towns as Stutton, Duxford, Cambridge, Felixstowe, Diss, Newmarket, Sudbury and Mildenhall. Only very rarely did any member of the Godric C.C. take part in these massed-start events.

The Diss and District C.C., for instance – the first sponsored club in East Anglia, because the Delite accessories firm had its headquarters in the town – promoted an afternoon of round-the-houses criteriums in midsummer of 1975. There were five separate races, from schoolgirls to seniors. In all, 223 cyclists took part in these races, but the programme reveals that there were only three entries from the Godric, and the riders from the Bungay club were all juniors.

A Club-run leaves the Butter Cross, early 1970s

In a moderate time-trialing year Geoff Mayne and Kevin Norman continued their genial contests. Godrics were now more inclined to travel to faster courses. Mayne and Norman rode the Cambridge University C.C. 25, and on the fast F2 Cambridge–St Neots road, Mayne did a 1.1 and Norman a 1.3. The quickest time that day was a 56 and ten riders were under the hour. These figures put the Godric challenge into perspective. The club was not disgraced, but its strongest riders found it hard to adapt to the new ways of dragstrip testing.

They were more used to the East Anglian courses on single-carriageway roads with exposed and windy conditions. Dragstrip riders would have avoided such a course as the NCA 100 on Breckland roads around the open spaces of Mildenhall Air Base, or the undulating and windswept Godric 25 Course on the A140 between Scole, Long Stratton and Tasburgh. In 1975 Pat Sheppard made a profitable journey south to take part in the Eagle R.C. 50. His ride made him a likely winner of the club BAR, though he was defeated by Lindsay Wigby's performance in the West Suffolk Wheelers 12. As so often, the Godric BAR Championship was decided by this event. For this and many other reasons there have always been most cordial relations between the Godric C.C. and its somewhat distant neighbours, who are based in Bury St Edmunds.

Pat Sheppard, 1975

In 1975 an especially local celebration was the Bungay Hog Fair. It was the revival of a nineteenth-century tradition. The Hog Fair was described in these words by Adrian Bell, who had wandered through Ditchingham Meadow in search for copy for his column 'A Countryman's Notes':

A youth was pedalling frantically a racing bicycle, which stayed where it was, being on rollers. This represented the Godric Cycling Club. Was Godric a cycling Saxon? 'How far do you go for a day's outing?' I asked. 'To Harrogate, perhaps. You should join us …' I gazed on press pictures of tours and road races: at the all-fours creature a cyclist becomes on those spider-web wheels. Yes, there is something heroic about them; and such expressions of grit, or agony, or of triumph riding past the winning post, hands held high. 'Do you ever get off for a hill?' 'Never'.

This must be the only time that the Godric C.C. has featured in *The Times*. The nostalgic author of *Corduroy* (1936), obviously thought that racing cyclists were a peculiar modern curiosity. Other local people knew better. As we have continually seen, the Godrics were a familiar and valued part of the Bungay community.

Why did the young man on rollers mention Harrogate? Probably because he had been on the recent ESCA/Godric touring expedition to Yorkshire, which included a visit to the Harrogate Festival of Cycling. As for the question of dismounting for hills … Mr Bell should have made an expedition to the club's hill-climb, held this year on Long Lane Hill, Stoke Holy Cross. A new young Godric took the prize – one of Phillip Bellerby's numerous wins that season.

Lindsay Wigby was the Godric's representative in the N.C.A.'s hill-climb championship on Roman Camp Hill, Aylmerton. It is 900 yards long and Norfolk's highest point above sea-level. After half a lifetime in this branch of cycle sport, Lindsay Wigby probably knows more about hill-climbs than anyone else in East Anglia and, as so often happens, this specialist hill-climber was also good on grass. In 1975 Wigby had already shown his talents in every aspect of the bike game. He was the club's 50 champion and BAR. At the club dinner he was awarded the Memorial Rose Bowl (voted on privately by all members) which thanks a person with the best all-round services to the Godric C.C. The award was all the more touching because it is given in memory of Lindsay Wigby's mother, Edna.

x   x   x   x   x

At the end of 1975 there were 51 members of the Godric. Most of the club's activities were successful, and funds stood at £78.89. On the other hand, attendance at club runs continued to be patchy. At various times, and to the present day, there have been various attempts to revive the club run tradition. It will never wholly die, for the simple reason that one of the delights of cycling is to ride in company. Many Godrics meet informally, either on Wednesdays (Bungay's early closing day) or Sunday mornings, though without a recognised meet at the Butter Cross. The runs-list was replaced by telephone arrangements, and plans are made either at the clubroom or at the Godric's favourite café, the Butter Cross Tea Rooms, which is also a place of rendezvous for members of other clubs.

The club-run could not be wholly revived. Nor was there a real future for the former Godric speciality, roller racing. In the 1950s there had been a number of events of this sort throughout East Anglia, and some show of strength or style on the rollers was often a feature of 'Champions' Night' at the Albert Hall. Roller racing seems less nonsensical if it takes place on a platform, if its audience has never seen it before and if some record is being attempted. Therefore, the Godric provided some entertainment at the Bungay Hog Fair.

In a distant time – 1968 – the Godric had set a four-man 12-hour roller record with a combined distance of 508 miles. The team was Adrian Perkin, John Pugh, Bernard Trudgill and Lindsay Wigby. Their feat was given an entry in the *Guinness Book of Records*. At the Hog Fair of 1976 another roller team (Phil Bellerby, Phil Brown, Geoff Mayne and John Pugh) increased the former mileage to 576. Their success encouraged the club to purchase a set of four competition rollers and a clock. The cost was £350 – quite a challenge to club funds.

A more economical venture, and a race that brought friends to the Godric C.C., was the 1976 promotion of the National Veteran's Cyclo-Cross Championship. It was mainly the work of Lindsay Wigby, who devised a difficult course that gave a first sight of Broome Heath to crossmen from as far away as Bradford, London and Birmingham. Graham Bufton was the winner.

A film, which has not survived, was made of this race. Major survivors of the 1976–7 cross season should be mentioned. They were the Godric junior team of Richard Avery, Simon Dawson, Terry Doughty and Kevin Mayne. All of these juniors were set on the path of future distinction in road-racing. But how were they to learn about cycle sport? Who would guide and inspire them?

The record-breaking roller team: (left to right)
John Pugh, Bernard Trudgill, Lindsay Wigby, Adrian Perkin

41

The E.S.C.A. ride from Land's End to John O'Groats:
(right to left) Geoff Mayne, Wendy Page, John Denson,
Kevin Mayne, Dale Clarke, Richard Avery, Andy Warne,
Terry Doughty, Graham May, Geoffrey Leggett

CHAPTER 9

These racing juniors were no doubt among the audience at an 'Any Questions' evening that began the 1977 season. There was a good panel. It consisted of Mick Gambling, Norwich journalist, short-distance time-trialist and coach; Steve Lawrence, the young international; Eddie Taylor, organiser of most racing activities at Haverhill; and Derek Buttle, former Hercules professional and Tour of Britain rider, who had moved to Suffolk and joined the Godric.

Most of the questions were about training, diet, choice of gears and similar topics. These matters are discussed by all cyclists, whenever they meet: but it was helpful to hear some experts. Training advice within the Godric was not particularly sophisticated. Most people trained harder by doing more and more miles, alone or in one of the groups that made fast circuits of the 'Homersfield Round' or the Bungay–Beccles–Bungay loop on the northern and southern sides of the river.

In the BCF East Anglia Junior Road Championship the Godric team was Richard Avery, Dale Clarke, Simon Dawson and Kevin Mayne. These riders, together with Terry Doughty, and Andrew and Patrick Warne, would be the future generation of the club's racing men. But they were very young, certainly not ready to match the old masters of time-trialing, Geoff Mayne and Roly Stevenson, who ruled over the longer distances.

The differences in their ages were extreme. Stevenson had been a veteran for some time and Mayne passed his fortieth birthday this season: while the Godric entries in the Norwich A.B.C. city-centre races (Richard Avery, Dale Clarke, Simon Dawson, Kevin Mayne and Wendy Page) were not even in the junior race, but started off the afternoon's festivities in the schoolboys/girls event.

Most of these young people took part in the dramatic E.S.C.A. ride from Land's End to John O'Groats. The teenagers covered the 875 miles in 44 hours and 50 minutes. Officially, they represented Bungay High School. The Godric C.C. may claim them, since they were all young members. Richard Avery, Dale Clarke, John Denson, Terry Doughty, Kevin Mayne, Andrew Warne and reserve Wendy Page rode in relays. After every ten miles each rider handed the baton to the next, so each member of the team covered about 146 miles during the end-to-end marathon.

There was an elaborate back-up team with a minibus and a support van from the Beccles firm of J. W. Leggett. The young people, who had to sit for hours in slow-moving vehicles, relished their opportunities to get out and sprint away on a bike. A long-winded way to prove that cycling is more pleasant than motoring, some might argue; but it was a great adventure, thanks to Geoff Mayne, and also introduced Graham May, a Bungay High School fourth year tutor, to cycle sport and to the Bungay club.

The Godric has a well-deserved reputation for hospitality, and not only because so many cyclists like to visit the unique town of Bungay, and ride the lanes and ancient highways of north Suffolk. The club's cyclo-cross events are always popular and so are its open events. In 1977 there was the usual open 25 on an August Sunday morning that had been preceded by an open 10 on Saturday afternoon. Seventy-seven cyclists rode the 25, and 69 rode the 10. That was a good field. Was it possible that Bungay and the Godric were on the brink of a new era? An optimistic Lindsay Wigby wrote that Bungay 'that sleepy little market town that nestles on the Norfolk/ Suffolk border had been in a state of decay according to the sages ever since the cattle market closed. Suddenly hey presto and its all happening, with two pubs reopening, a Chinese take-away and several other shops reopening … amongst them has appeared Roy's Bike Shop … The proprietor is our own Roy Mobbs who has attractively decorated this small shop with racing news and posters…'

x   x   x   x   x

As we have seen, the Godric has been a 'family club'. So are many cycling clubs, though at the beginning of the twenty-first century there are fewer of them; and in the Godric itself fewer members are now related by blood or by marriage. In earlier days wheels were often held aloft by clubmates as the bride and groom left a local village church. Marriage (and, sometimes, divorce) is part of the complicated network or relations within a club devoted to cycling and to fellowship. These are personal matters. But the club's history should mention some of the Godrics who became married, or who were brought up under the same roof.

After George and Daphne King (who obviously had a parental role in the birth of the club) the oldest Godric families are the Maynes, the Wigbys and the Stevensons, leaders of club life since its earliest youth and still active today, half a century later. As noted above, there were six Godric marriages before 1961. Family connections probably became more important in the 1970s. They reached a height in the 1978 season – which began a few weeks after a dinner at which Kevin Mayne made his maiden speech in toasting the visitors.

As the 1978 season proceeds, we note the efforts of (in the junior section) Andrew Warne and his younger brother Patrick, then Terry Doughty and his younger brother Garry. Their cousins were Daphne and Wendy Page, whom we have already met. Then we find, in the club's 25, the popular Chairman Ron Howell racing against his son Stephen. In the same race were more brothers: Kevin and Trevor Mayne; Michael, John and Keith Denson; and John and Robert Riches (whose father Maurice in this year was awarded the Edna Wigby memorial trophy for his work as the Clubroom Secretary).

Terry Doughty

Later in the 1978 season we meet two more pairs of brothers: Robert and Stephen Catling, and Simon and Martin Dawson. Beside all these siblings, family dynasties continued. Roy Mobbs introduced his daughter Lesley to cycle sport. The veteran Jimmy Smith rode with his daughter Caroline, who was to marry a fellow Godric, Jeremy Wentford, and as Caroline Wentford was the Godric C.C.'s Secretary in the 1990s.

In 1978 Maureen Wigby took over the Secretary's duties from Doreen Stevenson. A cash-book from this period records attendances and donations at club nights. As we would expect, many family names are repeated, week after week. Then, some names are missing both from the records of club nights and from racing records. Eighteen year olds were leaving Bungay for higher education. In the late 1970s there was the first exodus of bright students who left the region for universities elsewhere in the country. They preferred Sheffield, Birmingham and Newcastle to London, which in actual fact is closer. The metropolis was not attractive. In any case, not many of them returned to competitive cycling in the Bungay area.

Steve Catling, 1980

The exodus of young cyclists from the region was not quite equalled by the arrival of older wheelmen, who on the whole came from London. They were either retired or had relocated to the Bungay neighbourhood because of new employment opportunities in an attractive rural setting. In this way the Godric combination of being a very young persons' club and an old persons' club took a new turn. The vintage Godric families, those mentioned above, became the link between the newcomers and local teenagers. It is also probable that ex-Londoners felt young again when cycling in the Waveney Valley; and there is further evidence that the newcomers, though of advanced years, were likely to join a number of community organisations – as retirement hobbies, or because they wished to be a genuine part of local life.

So it is helpful to look at a prospectus of local voluntary societies, listed for a gathering at the Beccles Public Hall in September of 1978. In all about 50 religious, social, sporting, cultural and political groups were represented. The Godric C.C. had its place beside other sporting clubs as well as associations concerned with, for instance, fishing, light opera, gardening and cage birds. Cycling clubs in big towns or cities have never been interested in this sort of participation. They keep to themselves. But the Godric C.C. was a visible and natural part of Waveney life.

In Bungay, community relations would now be especially relevant. At the club dinner in early 1979 the guests included Sergeant A. C. Dack. He spoke of the good relations between racing cyclists and the police who were responsible for road safety. Sergeant Dack had been carefully invited to the dinner, for the Godric C.C. was now planning to promote a series of Bungay criteriums on Whit Monday. The club wished to close Lower Olland Street, Wingfield Street, part of Beccles Road and Wharton Street. Police permission was essential. So was the help of the St John's Ambulance Brigade, the goodwill of local tradesmen and the co-operation of residents who lived on the course.

As it turned out, tradesmen and shopkeepers liked the idea of cycle-racing. From their point of view, Bungay had always seemed a 'dead town' on the Bank Holiday. All went well, though the weather was not kind. There was a festive atmosphere in the town and the winner of the senior race was the London international rider Bob Downs. He asked if he could come again next year. And so a tradition was born, out of the hard work of Lindsay and Maureen Wigby.

Prize-winners at a club dinner, late 1970s

Action in the May Day races

CHAPTER 10

In a chilly spring the May Day criteriums warmed the hearts of all Godrics and their friends but also pointed to a weakness in the club. As before, Godrics were seen in the junior races but no one from the promoting club had entered the senior event. Time-trialing was still the major racing activity. Since this branch of the sport has few spectators it must have been remote from the townspeople of Bungay who, in May, had seen road-racing for the first time. So the club was fortunate that its doings were so well reported by local newspapers, in particular the *Beccles and Bungay Journal* and the *Eastern Daily Press.*

This was a fruitful year for Godric time-trialing. It was especially good for Kevin Norman. He began the year by setting a record for the Earsham–Billingford 25 course with a 1.2.38. This relatively slow time shows how difficult and 'sporting' the local courses were. Norman then rode a 56.25 on the classic fast course at Sandy in Bedfordshire. He was half-way up the listings in the National Championship 25, held in 1979 on a course between Bury and Newmarket; and then he claimed another Godric record with a 55.47 in the Redbridge C.C. promotion.

In this year Cyril Wigby was in competition for the first time since 1939. Together with Doreen and Roly Stevenson he was invited to a Breckland C.C.10. The event had been devised as a gesture of thanks to all the timekeepers, marshals and other officials who had selflessly helped the cause of East Anglian cycle sport. For once, it was the young champions who did the paperwork, held the watch, made the tea and kicked their heels at the side of distant roundabouts. Cyril even won the event!

The membership of the Godric C.C. at the end of 1979 was 97, the highest ever. It was inevitable, and perhaps fortunate, that the number should decrease. A very large number of subscriptions leads to an unwieldy club whose members might not even know each other. Then there is the danger of a split. But the Godric was never divided. Some members left because their interests changed, or they went to university, or because their jobs took them away from Bungay. Others joined nearby clubs such as the Waveney Valley R.C. and the V.C. Baracchi or the Lowestoft Wheelers. It should be said that in the Norwich area the clubs were more volatile, and some of them have had short lives.

A friendly club was – and is – the Diss and District C.C. Among its members was Geoff Banham, who now did a good turn to the Godric – the first of many. He was good at finding sponsors for cycle events. The Godric enjoyed goodwill but lacked expertise in raising money from local firms.

It looked as if the second edition of the May Day criterium racing would not take to the Bungay streets, since the costs could not be met solely from Godric funds. Geoff Banham helped to solve the problem. Sponsors were found and the May Day races went ahead, to everyone's satisfaction.

x   x   x   x   x

Former schoolboy rider Richard Avery began the year with 50-mile training rides in the company of Kevin Norman. Then, on an early season wet and windy morning, he did a 1.1.46 on the Ipswich–Bury road, a time he soon reduced to 1.0.16. Avery, eighteen years old, was an engineering apprentice. He excelled with a series of 23-minute tens. These performances would bring him the evening events trophy. Dale Clarke, who was also eighteen in 1980, decided to concentrate on longer distances. He took his second club BAR after a win in the championship 50, a fast 100 and then a 221 in the West Suffolk Wheelers 12, despite injuring his foot when a car forced him off the road.

At the end of 1980 his clubmates also applauded the quiet but powerful and stylish riding of Pat Sheppard. When the new veteran arrived in Bungay the club gained not only a wise member but an expert on massage and other aspects of sports physiotherapy. In years to come the smooth organisation of many club events, both sporting and social, would depend on Pat Sheppard's efforts.

At this period the Godric was at last forming a road-racing team. The pioneering roadmen were Richard Avery, Robert Catling and Patrick Warne. The latter two riders showed well in the third of the annual May Day races, whose senior criterium had attracted such a rider as the amateur road champion Steve Lawrence. Later in 1981 the Godrics also rode in the Norwich city-centre races and the Diss 'round-the-houses' races. The outstanding feat was Richard Avery's first place in the C.C. Breckland's 60-kilometre event on a course based at Watton.

Another marvellous racing morning should be placed in the annals of the Godric. Three lads in the club colours went to the Essex/Suffolk Border Combine 25. Kevin Norman won the event in 55.43. Richard Avery beat the hour with a personal best and came 4th. Robert Catling went under the 60-minute barrier for the first time and came 2nd in the handicap section. These three riders took the team prize. They were supported by Patrick Warne and by Roly Stevenson, who recorded a 1.2.5., only three seconds short of his personal best.

There was more excellent time-trialing on the course between Ipswich and Bury. Richard Avery, Dean Clarke and Kevin Norman led the way. They were joined by an excellent schoolgirl rider, Caroline Smith. In the last two years a number of powerful new stars had emerged. An elder brother often led a younger. Dale and Dean Clarke, the teenagers from Homersfield, were prominent in the evening events. The club's handicap 25 gave Robert Catling a course and event record: one that could never be challenged, since the construction of the Harleston bypass meant that the Godric's old course would have to be redrawn and remeasured. On a different course, as the season ended, Kevin Norman once more reduced the club 25 record. He returned to the timekeeper with a 55.16.

*Patrick Warne, Caroline Smith and Jim Smith,
after the West Suffolk Wheelers 100, 1984*

The prominent members of the club at the beginning of 1982 can easily be seen in the awards given at the twenty-ninth annual dinner. Cyril Wigby, 69, was made an honorary member with a special presentation.

The prize-winners were Kevin Norman, for both the 50-mile Championship and the fastest 25. He shared another award with Dale Clarke, who had an equal number of points in the evening events competition. Caroline Smith won both the novices' trophy and the ladies' trophy. Robert Catling was junior BAR. John Pugh was given the club-runs president's trophy. Dave Hatcher was the best club member. Dean Clarke was junior track champion and Richard Avery senior track champion.

Lester Curtis had gained most points in the Silver Leaf competition. Roly Stevenson was recognised for the most meritorious performance of the season. Robert and Stephen Catling won, respectively, the 175 Trophy and the Riches Trophy. Lindsay Wigby claimed the Gong Trophy and Richard Avery was hill-climb champion.

Although most of them had been donated, the cost of these trophies and their engraving was always a worry to the club's Treasurer. The Godric funds could be described as generally adequate, but seldom ample. They would not cover an emergency. If, for instance, the hire of the village hall at Ditchingham became much more expensive (as happened in 1982), then the annual cyclo-cross event was at risk. It had been held for sixteen years and had become a target for every East Anglian crossman.

Fortunately, the Ditchingham problem was overcome. But financial problems never disappear. Considering finances, as they were bound to do, committee members of the Godric looked to other ways of making money. There were subscriptions: but these were not high and for the many young members not high at all: they could join for a shilling or two. Occasionally there were jumble sales. In years past there had even been a waste-paper collection. The annual dinner could either make a profit or a loss. There were raffles in the clubroom and entry fees to help defray the costs of organising races. But was this enough? Barely.

Evening 10s on the Halesworth road were not expensive to promote and in many ways were the bread and butter of the Godric's racing members. The May Day races were far more complicated and costly. Yet they had quickly become the club's showpiece. In 1981 the third of these celebrations attracted 120 entries. New events were added to the programme. There was a one-lap Soapbox Derby in aid of local charities, for instance. And then there was a criterium for tricycles, a rare treat for the barrow boys, for they normally competed only in time trials.

In a malevolent wind with flurries of snow the tricyclists (winner: Mick Madgett, Diss and District C.C.) showed their cornering skills to a smaller crowd than had been expected. But the various criteriums brought much enjoyment. The May Day celebrations would obviously continue. Once again, the Godric C.C. had found 'instant tradition', and had done so with the aid of local bodies that included the Bungay Area Lions Club and the businesses that were (and are) the backbone of the Lions enterprise. A long list of appreciations at the back of the 1982 programmes shows that the Godric took much from the generosity of Waveney Valley commerce. In another way they repaid that generosity, since the club devised other events – in particular the Cyclathon – whose proceeds were given to charity.

CHAPTER 11

In the summer of 1983 Lindsay Wigby was awarded the Bungay Town Council's Bezant Trophy, an honour given to the person who had made the greatest contribution to local sport. As was said at the ceremony, the Godric veteran had organised cyclo-cross events on Broome Heath for sixteen years. His most recent work had been in the May Day criteriums. In 1983 the Bungay Spring Bank Holiday races had made a profit for the first time. In previous years the Godric had lost around £50 every time the races were held. This year the club added £23 to its funds.

The turnaround in the finances of the May Day criteriums helped the way to a new venture. It was the Cyclathon, whose profits would be given to charity (cancer research, initially). The idea for the Cyclathon came from another local organisation, the Bungay Black Dog Running Club. The athletes organise a marathon which attracts entries from the locality and all the East Anglian region. Geoff Mayne competed in the 1983 marathon and reflected that it is much easier to ride 100 miles than to run 25 miles. He then devised a course of 25 miles in length that would start and finish in Bungay, and would be covered four times by the more committed wheelmen, or just once by family groups or cyclists who preferred an easy excursion. It was not a race. Finishers could claim a medal or a certificate. This original circuit took riders from Bungay to Flixton, Homersfield, Mendham, Withersdale, Metfield, Linstead, Halesworth and thence back to Bungay. In recent years the course has been changed to avoid traffic on the Halesworth–Bungay road. Thus the ride became hillier and even more rural. The course now turns eastward at Chediston, climbs, descends to Wissett, climbs again to Rumburgh, and then threads through the lanes before joining the main road for the final miles to headquarters at the Bungay Sports Centre.

Golden memories of the Cyclathon, which has been a yearly event since 1983, are shared by hard-riders, leisure cyclists and children who have made an extended bike trip for the first time. That is because the Cyclathon is so welcoming and its course so varied. Every mile or two brings a new physical experience, a different vista, a fresh challenge and the occasional opportunity to relax.

There are long, flattish sections, as on the road between Flixton and Homersfield; or intriguing corners, as the course winds through Mendham and gives sudden and lovely views of the Waveney. There are climbs, not severe, but hilly enough for two changes of gear and an effort out of the saddle. Above Metfield is high, open country, where aeroplane runways built during Hitler's war are laid on the ground like giant crucifixes; then a thrilling descent toward Linstead, where a lively rider would expect to be 'motoring'; followed by narrow lanes through woods and baffling changes of direction as roads skirt ancient fields towards a high point with a distant view of Bungay's church tower.

How difficult is this ride? As hard as you care to make it. A moderately fit adult cyclist, riding alone, neither hastening nor lingering, would expect to complete the circuit in about 1 hour and 30 minutes. It is always emphasised that the Cyclathon is not a race – but everyone knows that the experience of speed on a bike always makes one wish to be faster, and many Godrics vie with each other as the Cyclathon unfolds.

Riders in the first Cyclathon

The heart of any cycling club must be in the fellowship of its members, and perhaps the soul of a club is in shared memories of favourite roads. The Cyclathon course is used for training by the Godric's racing members and by all other cyclists, whether they be tourists, old-timers or family groups, for the delight of exploring north Suffolk, when maybe the goal of a ride is to visit a village church, or to linger in a country pub, or to see snowdrops, or bluebells, or to gather the ripened blackberries of late September, dark and sparkling as the polish of a hearse.

And yet, for so many Godric members, every mile of these familiar roads will stir memories of intense racing effort. For our ride begins on the old 25 course that followed the river valley toward Harleston; and it is half of the 'Homersfield Round' (nine miles, 1200 yards from Bungay, and back) occasionally used for time-trialing; then the Cyclathon route follows, pretty closely, the course of the Godric C.C.'s first road-race, criticised by some riders, in those faraway days, as being too rustic and tricky; and, finally, the run home on the 'Bungay Straight' is, of course, the historic setting of the club's 10-mile time trials.

In the early twenty-first century it is strange to think that, as recently as 1983, this 10 course on the Halesworth road was still used for time trials, the turn marshal standing in the middle of a quiet highway. The recollection is also saddening, since it is clear that motor traffic is destroying the sport of time-trialing; and from now on we will have to commemorate a number of Godrics and their friendly rivals from other clubs who have been injured or killed in road accidents.

What an accident is, only God can know. Cyclists, the most innocent of road-users, can only learn to grieve.

Philip, 'Pip' Curtis was a shy boy when he first became a Godric. He waited with his bike on the other side of the street as a club-run left the Butter Cross one Sunday morning. Then he tagged on behind the friendly riders and asked if he could join the club. Of course he was welcomed. Pip soon became loved within the club. The Godric brought out the charm of his character and innate high spirits. He in turn loved the club he had joined, became a youthful committee member, was briefly in the RAF C.C. when he became an airman, then was glad to win the Godric hill-climb Championship in the old green and gold colours. Pip was killed in a car crash at Acle in 1984. Rest in Peace.

Wendy Page, the Godric schoolgirl champion of former years, died in a car crash in Southern Spain in 1987. Many of her clubmates were present at the memorial service in Holy Trinity Church, Bungay. Rest in Peace. In the same year George King, the founder of the Godric C.C., died at the age of 63. His legacy remains and flourishes. Rest in Peace.

*Lindsay Wigby,
winner of the
Bezant Trophy*

*Pip Curtis
riding a hill-climb,
1982*

CHAPTER 12

Between 1982 and 1984 the Godric's hallowed time-trialing courses were replaced by new routes. The 25 course now used the Harleston bypass. It was christened in April of 1982, when Patrick Warne won with a 1.6.4. The innovatory 10 course started at Homersfield and turned at Ditchingham. Roundabout turns were welcomed by all. The only criticism of the new courses was (and is) that they are extremely windy – even, some say, when conditions are perfectly calm a mile or two away from the main road.

In the spring and summer of 1982 the Warne brothers were prominent in the 'Homersfield Round' races, together with Dale and Dean Clarke, Richard and Stephen Catling, Lindsay Wigby (often on his trike) and, among the ladies, Caroline Smith, and an energetic newcomer, Christine Colman. The club 50 championship was won by Kevin Norman, who was regularly posting excellent winning times in the early 1980s. Norman became club Chairman, and in January of 1984 the weekly magazine *Cycling* suggested that his personal best of 55.22 probably made him 'the fastest chairman in the country'.

General Secretary Ron Howell often had to work on Sundays but still managed to record the best attendances at the club-runs, while also showing his veteran's know-how in many a time-trial. Both in local and national time-trialing, the 25 was still a classic distance. On Suffolk courses, which on the whole are slower, the target was still to beat the hour. Barry Minns and Geoff Mayne had gone 'under' in the 1950s. In later years these two pioneers had been joined by Richard Avery and Kevin Norman. In 1982 four more Godric riders broke the barrier. They were Dale Clarke, Dean Clarke, Philip Curtis and Patrick Warne. Far away on a Harrogate course, Durham University student Kevin Mayne also went under the hour in the summer of 1983.

$$x \quad x \quad x \quad x \quad x$$

As 1983 ended, the year's major achievement appeared to have been the Cyclathon. Around 200 people, of all ages and standards, had been attracted to the event. They paid a small entrance fee and many of them were sponsored. Later in the year Kevin Norman, as club Chairman, was able to present a cheque for £1750 to the 'Big C' appeal. The large sum reflects the considerable amount of work that had been done organising the little tour of north Suffolk. Geoff Mayne, who had other commitments, was not sure that he could devote any more time to the event that he had invented.

In 1984 Pat and Margaret Sheppard took over. They received entry forms from 264 cyclists, including a team from Yorkshire.

At the club dinner local councillor John Palin presented the prizes and also read a poem he had written about the Godric:

> For 31 years they've been in the town –
> A cycling club of local renown.
> With cyclo-cross, time trials, rollers and racing
> The members have worked, new records they're facing.
> The veterans and juniors work side by side
> To uphold the club that's worthy of pride.
> On Sundays you'll find them, out in the air –
> They used to meet by the Market Square
> But now you'll see them, some time after 8
> Pedalling their bikes along the Halesworth Straight
> The May Day races, we're all justly proud
> This sporting event, attracting a crowd.
> To Bungay they come, from all over Britain
> A credit to Godric, much praise is befitting …

Mr Palin's verses imply that the club-runs that left the Butter Cross on Sunday mornings belonged to the past. This may have been so. The tradition was certainly coming to its end. The final club runs list in the Godric newsletter announced venues for October and November of 1983. The expeditions were to the Hill-Climb, the Broome Heath cyclo-cross meeting and the carol service at Pulham St Mary. Other runs were to Pakefield Beach, Walberswick and Peasenhall.

The club-run was disappearing all over the country. Social factors were no doubt to blame. Fewer cyclists combined racing and touring: in an age of specialisation they did one thing or the other. Young people did not like the time-honoured ethos of the run, whose gentle pace would be set by a leader or captain. There was no appetite for visits to monuments. The old cyclists'cafés were closing down. In any case, long halts in tea places occupied too much time on a Sunday, when there were other things to do. Both television and D.I.Y. hastened the demise of the club-run. Many cyclists did their 60–70 miles on a Sunday morning, without stopping, so that they would be home by the middle of the day. Their wives and children also preferred this arrangement.

x x x x x

Ron Howell (left) and Roly Stevenson

By their nature, club runs are the undramatic pastime of old, familiar friends. They have no commercial purpose. By 1985 (midway through Mrs Thatcher's premiership) the spirit of the age demanded financially successful activities. This was also the period of 'fun runs', mass participation in charitable ventures and the 'heritage industry', which aimed to make money from anything that was old. The Waveney Valley had its own way of contributing to these developments. As the *Beccles and Bungay Journal* often noted, there was a new mood of entrepreneurship in its rural area. Bungay celebrated itself, and helped local traders with the Hog Fair and plans for Victorian street-fairs, antique-fairs and the like, which became all the more numerous toward the end of the 1980s.

High on the list of these Bungay festivities were the Black Dog marathon (first held in 1982) the Cyclathon and the Godric's May Bank Holiday round-the-town races. Among the cycling fraternity these events gave Bungay the reputation of being a cycling town as, in truth, it was. Yet there was little direct benefit to the Godric C.C., if we think in either financial or sporting terms. The Godric put on May races for other people, since so few members of the club were themselves riders in the criteriums. The organisation was a matter of disinterested hospitality.

Lindsay Wigby, now himself a shop-owner, found it difficult to find time for work on the May holiday races, which he and Maureen Wigby had always organised. There was a danger that the seventh of the series, which took place in 1985, might be the last. The 1986 races were, in fact, cancelled, to everyone's dismay; and then, to everyone's deight, were saved. Once again it was Geoff Banham, local baker and snooker-hall owner, who came to the club's rescue.

He realised that the May criteriums should not take a year 'out'. There would be problems in having the road closed after a gap. The Bungay celebrations might slip from the racing calendar. Continuity was essential. So the races survived and to this day have brought a festive note to the racing season. In 1987 there were 130 entries in four races, with 40 riders competing in the senior event.

Young Keith Denson was the only one of these competitors in a Godric jersey, and rode in the popular tricycle event. Keith was to be an important part of the new profile of Godric racing, especially in time-trialing. Suddenly, both the start- and the results-sheets had a different appearance. New member Mike Horne, with twenty years experience of testing, rode a 58-minute personal best in mid-May and was impressive in the evening 10s. Paul Bedford, who had joined the Godric from the Lowestoft Wheelers, showed that he could beat Kevin Norman – a remarkable achievement – while Richard Cary concentrated on the longer distances, Jeremy Wentford tried all types of racing and connoisseurs of the bike game were already talking of a bright future for Andrew Caley, still a junior.

Bedford, Horne and Norman made a formidable trio, and took numerous team prizes in 1987. Bedford broke the Godric 50-mile record with a 1.52.49 on Essex roads. In the same Viking R.C. promotion Norman also registered a personal best with his 1.57.50. The season ended with Jeremy Wentford's win in the hill-climb. At the club dinner Richard Avery was awarded both the grass-track trophy and the 50 championship. Richard Cary won the 175 prize. In this year the Godric had organised 22 club time-trials and 2 open time-trials. In the August weekend there had been 70 entries for the Saturday afternoon 10, and 89 for the Sunday morning 25. In all, 350 cyclists had been involved in Godric time-trials. The club had also promoted numerous events on grass, together of course with the Broome Heath cyclo-cross, the Cyclathon and the May Day races.

It was a busy club and probably had never been busier. Yet the hard work was still done by the same people who had given their time and energies for so many years past. At the beginning of 1988 the chief officers were Lindsay Wigby, Chairman; Peter Bourchier, Vice-Chairman; Ron Howell, Secretary; Dave Hatcher, Treasurer; Doreen Stevenson, Racing Secretary. Needless to say, these officers were helped by husbands or wives. Roly Stevenson and Maureen Wigby must also have spent much time on paperwork while other club members wheeled the Norfolk and Suffolk lanes.

James Trenchard leading Shaun Aldous, May Day races

Record-breaking schoolboy roller team:
(left to right) Terry Doughty, Andrew Warne,
Richard Avery, Kevin Mayne, 1977

CHAPTER 13

The powerful Godric time-trialing team was less effective in the 1988 season. Paul Bedford was working in the south of England. Kevin Norman was interested in his second sport, road-running. Jeremy Wentford won the Handicap 25 early in the year. His wife Caroline (née Smith) took a number of prizes and was, of course, regarded by the Godrics as one of their own, though she was now in the colours of the Vegetarian A. & A.C. But Caroline Wentford was in a solitary position, either as a first- or second-claim member. Although its total membership now stood at 87 there were hardly any Godric women who raced.

Why was this? In the first place, young women no longer came to the club through the support and encouragement of the ESCA. Teenage girls were attracted to biathlon and triathlon events, which at the end of the 80s were a novel sporting (and social) enthusiasm. A Waveney Valley Triathlon Club, based at Beccles, was founded in 1987. Its first triathlon had 120 entries, a significant proportion of whom were women. Cycling is the most exciting of the triathlon disciplines. However, the Godric did not make converts from triathletes who had competed on a bike for the first time.

It was natural that girls should have been attracted to swimming rather than cycling. The activity was familiar, because everyone had swum at school. Bungay had a splendid new municipal pool. Furthermore, many parents would have thought, swimming is safer than cycling. It was obvious that the roads were becoming more dangerous. By 1988 there were no family-type Godric club-runs to lead a new cyclist towards confidence and the will to race. Bike-racing appeared a specialised sport, and was mysterious to outsiders.

Then – for people at entry level – there was the problem of equipment. Small front wheels, straight forks, cow-horn handlebars and disc back wheels had become almost obligatory within a couple of seasons. Mountain bikes seldom helped an aspiring teenage cyclist, though they were now used to good effect in Broome Heath cyclo-cross races. Off the road they are fun. On a metalled road mountain bikes are depressing after half an hour. It's like riding a tractor. They deprived young people of the extended thrill of long distances on a good racing machine.

Here were the difficulties for a girl, or any teenager, who had thought of becoming a cyclist. There are now the first signs that the Godric was becoming a club that belonged to its veterans. At the end of the 1980s, however, it was still a varied club, with a mixture of attitudes and a wide difference in ages. Attitudes can be guessed from members' machines, always a clue to the nature of a cyclist. Godrics used the classic clubman's bike, hand built and with gears for most purposes. In the winter many of them preferred to ride road/track machines with a fixed wheel. Younger time-trialists saved up for the 'funny bikes' that might make them faster on dragstrip roads. A number of members rode tricycles, both for pleasure and for racing, though they knew that they would record a slower time on three wheels. And one of the keenest 'barrow boys' was Keith Denson, who, as we have seen, was also one of the youngest club members.

The tricycle event in the Godric May Day criteriums is by no means a novelty race. It is probably the only criterium for three-wheeled bikes in the country, and is keenly contested. Year after year the race shows that the tricycle is part of cycling culture within East Anglia. People love to see it. But there were years when May Day cheering was subdued. On the morning of the 1988 races the brilliant young Andrew Caley was injured by a hit-and-run driver. Recovery took him a year. The Godrics clubbed together to buy Andrew equipment for his return to cycling and presented him with the gift at the annual dinner.

The public success of the May Day Races could be affected by the weather or an important football match on the television. This was obvious. But no one could say why the promotion was much more popular in some years than in others. In 1989 there were 180 entries, the highest ever figure. But the crowds were very thin. In this year the Godric also experienced a loss of interest in the Cyclathon. There were only 60 advance entries. Ninety people started, of whom 35 rode the full 100 miles. Fourteen months after the unknown motorist had so badly damaged his legs, Andrew Caley rode twice round the course to record 50 miles.

The Cyclathon organiser was Pat Sheppard, who was then 51 years of age. He was (and is) a dedicated time-trialist. Sheppard often travelled into Essex and Hertfordshire to compete on roads he had known as a young man. He had a liking for 30s – that beautiful distance, mostly appreciated by experienced connoisseurs of the time-trialing sport – but would ride many other events, as his work and other commitments allowed.

Here, for instance, is a week in the life of a busy racing clubman. In the seven days before the 1989 Cyclathon Pat Sheppard rode: first, a 10 on the Colchester road near Kelvedon, on Saturday afternoon; and then, on Sunday morning, the East Anglian Veterans' Championship 10, in which he finished high in the field of 80 riders; followed by, on Tuesday evening, the Godric club 10. He left the timekeeper at 7.10, finished, had a quick shower and then was at work at the Bungay Sports Hall, where he was a custodian, at 8 p.m. On Saturday Sheppard competed in the local 25 and on Sunday looked after the smooth running of the Cyclathon he himself had organised.

There are photographs of Pat Sheppard in competition in the 1989 season. He has his usual perfect position on the bike. He rode in an aerodynamic helmet and had a computer on the handlebars. On the other hand the photographs show that his machine was basically a road bike, probably 72 degrees parallel, with a double chainwheel and bosses for a down-tube feeding bottle. He used toe-clips and straps, fitted a pump and had a spare tubular behind the saddle.

In other words – here was a fast man who was not a slave to fashion, as Sheppard has remained. The same was true of the vast majority of the Godric's racing members, especially perhaps if they had pedalled past the barrier of 40 years on earth, cycling's division between senior and veteran riders. Prominent among the older cyclists in 1989 were the irrepressible 75-year-old George Coleman and three fast men in their early 40s, Barry Debenham (who coached his son Carl), Mike Horne (who often raced on a fixed wheel) and Graham Ward (who rode a super 12 this year and also introduced his daughter Sarah-Jayne to the sport).

In July, new member Chris Legood rode his first 25. He would now be often in the placings, together with his clubmates Richard Avery, Patrick Warne and Tony Yates. Late in the season Paul Bedford returned to familiar Suffolk and Norfolk roads, enjoyed his racing and must have been pleased with his 55.1 in a 25 on the A12 near Witham. Yet this ride has to be seen within its context. The event was won by Martin Pyne, the Norfolk time-trialist who has so often beaten not only the Godrics but also the members of every other East Anglian club. Pyne's time that morning was an astounding 50.1, the fastest of the year in the whole country, and only 37 seconds slower than the national competition record.

Sue Broadbent stoked by Charlie and Esme, 1995

*Lindsay, Stuart and
Maureen Wigby,
Cyclathon, 1990*

*Darren Main,
Cyclathon hero,
1991*

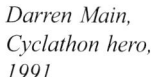

CHAPTER 14

True to the policy of friendly gestures toward other organisations, the Godric C.C. invited Mr E. Randall to speak at the annual dinner in February of 1990. Mr Randall was the representative of a younger cycling club, the V.C. Baracchi, based at Lowestoft. Replying to Graham Ward's toast to the visitors, Mr Randall praised the Godric and gave a number of reasons for the Bungay club's pre-eminent role in local cycling.

In a further contrast to other clubs, Mr Randall spoke of the Godric C.C.'s work for charities. In the previous few years the club had indeed raised thousands of pounds for good causes, mainly through the Cyclathon. These funds came through sponsorship, either of individual cyclists or of the event in which they were riding, and the money was then passed to cancer research, or a hospital, or Dr Barnardo's homes.

This practice was in direct contrast with the sponsorship that was sought by a number of other clubs. They hoped to receive money for their own purposes. Clubs approached commercial firms that wished to advertise. They added the firm's name to their own name and put an advertising logo on to fashionable road jerseys. In return, they often received help with transport costs to compete on speedy courses, and there were other benefits. However, sponsors wanted an undeserved place on the club's committee, the mutual arrangement rarely lasted for more than three or four years, ill feeling was often created and young racing cyclists were more likely to change their clubs.

Commercial sponsorship in British cycling began in the 1970s. By 1983 about 10 per cent of clubs affiliated to the BCF had involved themselves with advertising. Most, if not all, of them were in the larger towns or cities. And even in such a rural and idealistic club as the Godric there was a new mood. There were mutterings that the club was behind the times. It ought to have a more contemporary style, said some. We must keep to our traditions, said others. There was no clear path toward a more modern club, even if it were agreed that a change of character was desirable. Arguments about the future of the Godric usually focused on a redesign of the racing strip. Hardly anybody wished to belong to a sponsored club. Those who did took their own course.

$$x \quad x \quad x \quad x \quad x$$

In the bright late winter of 1990 the disappointment of the previous summer's Cyclathon was forgotten in a keen reliability trial – strangely, the club's first and last. Cyclathons were for anyone. Reliability trials are for committed cyclists who wish to test their legs after the close season. No fewer than 68 riders sped through the Saints on two laps of a 25-mile circuit, with the usual competition between groups at the front. Another well-attended winter occasion was the set of 'Come and Try It' cyclo-cross races on Broome Heath, devised by Geoff Banham. He had noticed the interest among spectators of the cyclo-cross championships in November and decided to attract anyone who might enjoy 'mud-plugging' as it was formerly called, cyclo-cross being the term used by most Godrics, while teenagers talked of mountain-bike racing and BMX.

Another diversion this winter was racing on the club's rollers. There was the annual club championship, special races for juveniles – in whose results the name of Shaun Aldous first appears – and a challenge match with the V.C. Baracchi, who were easily defeated. Roller racing is best performed before any large and inexpert audience. A team of four Godrics, Richard Avery, Chris Legood, Patrick Warne and Jeremy Wentford, set up their machines outside the Beccles Safeway for a stunt charity ride. In four hours, doing ten-minute stints, they covered 153 miles. There was another use for the Godric's set of rollers and clock. Every summer they were lent to the Norwich Cycling Association for the Outdoor Sports Stand at the Royal Norfolk Show.

The general state of Godric racing in the early season of 1990 can be seen in the various events over the Easter weekend. On the morning of Good Friday five Godrics rode the Great Yarmouth C.C. open 10 on the Earsham–Redenhall course. They were Mike Horne, Chris Legood, Pat Sheppard, Graham Ward and Tony Yates. Horne, Sheppard and Ward were veterans. In the afternoon of Good Friday the Lowestoft Wheelers' open 10 was held on the Homersfield–Ditchingham course. The competing Godrics were Richard Avery, Chris Legood and Graham Ward. On Easter Monday the East Anglian C.C. open 10 used the Hales–Redenhall course. The Godric entries were Richard Avery, Mike Horne, Chris Legood and Tony Yates. That morning Pat Sheppard travelled to Witham for the East Anglian Cycling Association veterans' 25. This was also the weekend of one of the 'Come and Try It' series of races on Broome Heath, notable for the performances by James and John Trenchard. In the club's evening 10s there were reliable performances by all the senior riders, a return to fitness by Andrew Caley, and some fast appearances by Shaun Aldous.

Paul Bedford returned from a lay-off in the later part of the 1990 season, as hard a competitor as ever he was. During his time with the club Bedford was by far the most successful Godric in races from 10 to 100 miles. His prowess against the clock emphasised that the club's first concern was time-trialing. At the May Day Races, only six Godrics appeared in a total entry of nearly 200 riders. Many people have puzzled over this lack of interest in massed-start racing. They look to the traditions of the region. The British League of Racing Cyclists, which set the pattern of post-war road-racing, was not strongly supported in East Anglia. So the BLRC had no legacy. Apart from round-the-houses races in Bungay, Diss and Norwich, often held at bank holiday weekends, there were not many events for an East Anglian roadman to enter. On the other hand the testing scene had a full calendar. A keen cyclist could race twice or even three times a week in Suffolk and Norfolk time-trials, and without travelling to the further ends of these counties.

Weight of tradition also helps to account for the survival of grass-track racing in the Waveney Valley area. In 1990 a writer in the *Beccles and Bungay Journal* lamented that 'with the advent of road-racing in this country, cycle-racing on grass, so popular 50 years ago, has almost died out in England …' This old-timer was reporting the Godric grass-track championships. They had formerly been held at the Bungay Hog Fair but were now contested, with a smaller audience, on the Bungay High School playing field. This is the moment to salute the achievement of Richard Avery. He was perhaps the last of the great East Anglian grassmen. In 1990 'Rik' won the 1000 Metres Challenge trophy for the tenth time, and at the end of the season recorded his eighth win in the Godric hill climb championship.

x   x   x   x   x

Even if it rains or snows, clubfolk always use their hill-climbs to celebrate the pleasure of being a cyclist. All around the country, the event marks the end of the racing year and the beginning of the social season. The Godric's short uphill trial has one sad aspect. The junior trophy (won in 1990 by the agile Shaun Aldous) is awarded in memory of Pip Curtis, a young man who was robbed of his life.

Youth and experience made a bond when Andrew Caley and Graham Ward rode from Land's End to John O'Groats (874 miles), taking a leisurely twelve days and collecting money for medical charities to which Andrew, the recent victim of a motor car, was indebted. And then they had the awkward journey from furthest Galloway back to Bungay …

It is curious that no Godrics have attempted a ride that begins on their home territory, the 390 miles (approximately) between England's and Wales' most eastern and western points – Lowestoft Ness and St David's in Cardiganshire. Maybe the complex journey south of Birmingham offers too squalid an experience. But, yet again, we see the power of local tradition. It is as though there is a barrier at the Great North Road – the A1 between London and York – that forbids East Anglian cyclists to venture into the Midlands and beyond.

Even in the twenty-first century, East Anglian cyclists can enjoy hundreds of miles of traffic-free roads. In 1991 a 'Sporting Courses' competition, which was a reaction from dragstrip racing, was extended to the counties of Cambridgeshire, Norfolk and Suffolk. To some extent, SPOCO events compensated for the lack of massed-start racing, and they made a welcome change from the A143. There was a popular circuit linking Gillingham with Haddiscoe and Hales, for 25 miles are covered if the route is ridden twice.

It was clear that other courses could be devised. One of them was a 25 route that led from Wrentham to Henstead and Frostenden, finishing on the straight at Kessingland. This course was invented by the V.C. Baracchi. Paul Bedford, a cycle mechanic by profession, used the race to give a first chance to his new tri-bars. Perhaps that is why he went off course on his local roads and covered perhaps 30 miles, while the winner of the event was Shaun Aldous, now increasingly confident in all types of cycle sport.

The club's new strip, 1992

CHAPTER 15

New courses and innovative equipment made very little difference to the essence of time-trialing. Non-cyclists find it difficult to grasp the nature of riding against the clock. You need to have done it yourself. Time-trialing is the most mysterious of British sports. There are few spectators apart from the marshals and the timekeeper sees even less of the event than those lonely clubfolk who stand, often for many hours, at junctions and roundabout turns. Furthermore, seeding ensures that the leading riders do not come into contact with each other, and a contestant may well finish his race before a rival has started.

Only time-trialists themselves can understand the physical effort and fiercely meditative concentration that are combined in a good ride. It is a private matter. Many if not most cyclists race in the knowledge that they will neither win nor enter the placings. They are interested in the personal experience of racing. The only prize they seek is a 'personal best', a time they have never previously achieved. One such cyclist – the Godric has known dozens of them – was Harry Hancy. In 1991 he returned to competitive cycling after many years and did a sequence of rides in the Godric 10s that were marked by tenacity on the bike, and good humour at the results board.

Personal-best rides often go unrecorded, but in 1991 sympathetic local journalists noted a number of these times. In an evening 10 (we read in the *Beccles and Bungay Journal*) Stuart Wigby – aged 12 – went off in the Number 1 slot. Number 2 was Harry Hancy – aged 68 – who caught Stuart just before the finish. Both went faster because they knew they were 'on a personal', as cyclists say. Other personal bests this season were achieved by Shaun Aldous, Chris Legood, James Trenchard and Graham Ward. The talented young Trenchard was having a marvellous year and may indeed have had a 'p.b.' nearly every time he rode. Apart from time-trialing, he showed well in the May Day criteriums and won a circuit race at Gorleston.

In September the Godric C.C. shared an afternoon of cycling and athletics with the Bungay Black Dog Running Club. Alas, there were few spectators. Godrics were pleased to see an old comrade, Kevin Norman, who this year won the Bezant Cup for services to sport in the Bungay area. Now, the Secretary of the Black Dogs, 33-years-old Kevin Norman had been a Godric member for 17 years and Chairman for four years. In his Bezant acceptance speech he said that 'Since my schooldays I realised that whatever club you are in there is a small nucleus of people willing to put in the time to run it, and unless you do it the club will lose its way.'

The 'small nucleus' of Godric officials still ran the club, and committee members would scarcely change until the end of the following year. The committee made everything possible for racing members and, they hoped, future generations of Godric stars. Three young men brought the season to a storming conclusion. In the ECCA 25 on the Cochester–Chelmsford road James Trenchard did a 54.11 in his last ride before his sixteenth birthday, leading Paul Bedford (54.54) and Shaun Aldous (57.10). After their brilliant performances in Godric colours Aldous, Bedford and Trenchard now joined another club, the V.C. Norwich.

x   x   x   x   x

At the 1991 Annual General Meeting in December, which was the thirty-seventh in the club's history, it was announced that the membership stood at 75. The Godric C.C. had promoted 26 time trials in the year and there had been 385 separate rides in the evening events. Within the committee there was a desire to revive the club's touring activities. Communal rides and club-runs were planned and it was decided to donate the profits from the next years Cyclathon to the Cyclists' Touring Club.

One or two papers carried the story that a local CTC official had conducted a house-to-house survey within Lowestoft and had found that more people in the town had access to a bicycle than to a car. The (probably inexact) statistic was part of a 'bike to work' campaign inaugurated by the CTC. The Godric C.C. had no especial interest in the way that people went to their employment. The club promoted cycling for pleasure, not excluding the pleasure of feats on the bike. Hats off to Darren Main, hero of the 1991 Cyclathon at the age of ten. Darren managed two circuits (50 miles) with his father Alistair, begged for more, then completed 75 miles and 100 miles before falling from his bike, triumphant, when he returned to the event headquarters at the Bungay Sports Centre.

This was one of the years when about the same number of people, 200, entered both the Cyclathon and the Godric time-trialing weekend held a few weeks later, which combined a 10 on Saturday afternoon and a 25 on Sunday morning. Looking through the Godric names on the start-sheets, one notices veterans such as Peter Bourchier and Harry Hancy. They were now joined in competition by Jim Caplin, formerly of the Kentish Wheelers, who in recent years had spent much of his leisure time at the end of a fishing rod. Caplin recovered all of his old enthusiasm when he put a number on his back most summer Sunday mornings. He was to become the editor of the Godric C.C.'s newsletter and at the club's fiftieth birthday dinner in

March 2003 was awarded the trophy for the most meritorious ride of the year.

At the beginning of 1993 there were changes in the former management of the Godric club. Ron Howell (so pleasantly assisted by his wife Grace) had been Secretary for eleven years. He now passed the post to Caroline Wentford. She was to be helped by Harry Hancy, who became Membership Secretary, and by Chris Legood, who attended every meeting in his role as Minutes Secretary. Cyril Wigby, Press Secretary for very many years, now retired, and was succeeded by Pat Sheppard. Shaun Aldous had become a second-claim member of his old club and offered to take on the post of Training Officer.

John Pugh with the Bezant Trophy

Jim Burgess

Geoff Mayne in his annus mirabilis

CHAPTER 16

Now began an unexpected development in the history of the Godric C.C. It was the surge of energy that belonged with maturity. Like a tide that retreats and then comes back to its native shore, three or four veterans returned to Godric racing. Geoff Mayne, after years when his profession had taken him to Sheffield, suddenly appeared at the first time trial of the 1992 season. He was 'looking lean' said the *Beccles and Bungay Journal,* continuing that 'riding with the same aggressive style as he did in the seventies, Mayne took top honours for the two laps of the Earsham–Hedingham circuit …'

Another writer noted that Mayne was riding 'a rather ancient track machine' in contrast to the state-of-the-art bicycles favoured by the riders he had beaten. John Pugh, who was in the same event, also preferred 1950s equipment (as he still does). Like Mayne, Pugh had been one of the earliest teenage Godric members. He had left Bungay to live in North Walsham, but was in touch with his old club and longed to return to competition. Nearly four decades after he first became a Godric, Pugh started a new training programme. It was based on a routine of 1,000 miles a month. He would soon be ready to challenge anyone and startled younger men with some zippy 25 times. Long-distance races, however, were to be Pugh's speciality.

As we know, the career of a racing cyclist can last for a lifetime. It is quite common for someone to begin as a teenager and still race at the age of 70 – or more! No other sport offers such longevity. Cycling also allows its devotees to return to racing after years of absence, being 'out'. Good clubs encourage the people who take their old bikes out of the shed after a period in the wilderness. The Godric has a good record with 'comebackmen'. They have been a part of the club almost from its earliest years.

In the 1993 season Mayne and Pugh made a team with Terry Doughty, who had been 'out' for some years after injuries caused by a hit-and-run driver. Doughty was 33 years old when he resumed his time-trialing career. He went under the hour at Easter, was consistently the fastest finisher in the evening 10s, became the club 50 champion later in the year, and closed his splendid season as club champion after a first place in the 1,000 metres grass-track race.

Other prominent riders in the 1993 season were Pat Sheppard (in his fortieth competitive season), Geoff Reeves, Tim Bonnett, Gavin Cole and young Julie Smith, who was also the cheerful organiser of gatherings at the clubroom on Maltings Meadow. Julie took a part in all aspects of club life and was certainly a voice in the discussions that, for week after week, took up the members' time. They concerned the vague but emotive issue of a new racing strip.

The club was 40 years old. Surely, argued some young members, it was time that the Godric had a more contemporary style. Others were cautious. They did not want change merely for the sake of fashion. Yet it was obvious that the yellow and red hoops on the old road jerseys had a dated look. Eventually it was agreed that there should be a new design. It was carried out by the Art Department of Bungay High School. The green, yellow and red colours (based on the arms of the Earls of Bigod) remained, but were redistributed, as though with the aid of an airgun, and with the addition of white. Skin suits quickly followed. Today, the original jerseys are sought by collectors.

Both old and new jerseys were worn at the inauguration of the Godric Way in November of 1993. This was a circuit of 24 miles through lanes around Bungay on both sides of the Waveney. It was modelled on the routes, almost always for pedestrians, that became common in the late 1980s and were intended to attract visitors to country towns. The circuit complemented the Bigod Way footpath network set up by the town council in 1987. Like many other 'town trails', walks, routes and 'ways', the Godric Way had a neat brochure and map, produced in collaboration with the town council.

The Godric Way heads east from Bungay toward Ellingham, crosses the river to Ditchingham and Hedenham, turns south-west to Earsham, Alburgh and Homersfield before returning to Bungay through the Saints. It is a delightful ride, except that the main A143 has to be traversed twice, and there is a dangerous right turn on the main Halesworth road at Ilketshall St John. These hazards discouraged young families and the complex circuit is inadequately signposted, except on the one day each autumn that the Godric members decide to ride the route.

Or some of the route, depending on mood. The Godric Way contains a paradox. Cycling is synonymous with freedom. The possession of a bike means that you can go wherever you like, either on roads that you love or through lanes that you wish to explore. Club cyclists do not wish to be told where to ride; and leisure cyclists who have holiday rides with their families scarcely ever become committed to a club.

x x x x x

Although the idea of the Godric Way brought little benefit to the club, the Cyclathon was almost always popular, especially in the benign weather of June 1995. As usual, more than 200 cyclists came to the starting line at the Sports Hall. For many of them it was one of their favourite annual events. Looking at the start sheet, one also finds newcomers among the bunches of riders who were sent on their way by Doreen Stevenson, and some of these newcomers would become devoted Godric members. Among them were Tim and Daniel Hilton (tandem), and Sue Broadbent who rode the course on a tricycle trailer bike, stoked by her children Charlie (5) and Esmé (3).

In the previous year Charlie and Esmé had been to cycle events in their mother's sidecar, a famous sight in Ditchingham and for miles around. Now they could flex their legs. Sue Broadbent also expanded her horizons. Between domestic duties she helped the Godric club in many ways and also began to race. In her first 'serious' year of racing, 2000, she was the fastest woman rider on fifteen occasions in open events, won the club's Ladies Trophy and was also made Sportswoman of the Year in a ceremony organised by the Waveney Sports Awards committee.

x   x   x   x   x

'Serious' racing in the later 1990s was often led by Geoff Mayne. Like many veterans, he was both an elder statesman and a cyclist with the enthusiasm of a youngster. So Mayne was in a double position. He had decided that he would shortly retire from the sport but wanted to make a flying exit. Now the Godric C.C.'s Chairman, Mayne trained hard, achieved some of his best times and also told his clubmates long stories about the exploits of 40 years before.

One of his tales concerned the club's 100-mile record. It stood to Barry Minns, long departed from the club and from cycling, who in 1958 had recorded a 4.17.28 on the A11 Norwich–London road. All these years later, Mayne encouraged Terry Doughty to break the record. After a heroic ride in the Norland 100 near Biggleswade, Doughty came home with a 36-second improvement on Minns' time. Geoff Mayne had witnessed both rides. He brought Minns and Doughty together for an interview and Press photograph, and was pleased to have acted as godfather to the continuity of Godric record breaking.

As if to prove that Doughty was still in the early part of his career, Mayne then broke the Godric veterans' 50 record. At the end of the 1995 season he also won the veterans' best all-rounder trophy. Veterans mattered to the Godric C.C. in many ways. Even if they had left the club and no longer rode a bike, there were now many local people who had fond memories of the days when they were young Godrics: and if they ran local businesses they were happy to sponsor the Bungay club's events.

Of all commercial enterprises in Bungay, the most friendly to the local cycling club must be the Butter Cross Tea Rooms. It is the unofficial headquarters of the Godric C.C., and became more important to club life as the popularity of the Maltings Meadow clubroom declined. A true cyclists' tea place of the old sort, the café is frequented by all Godrics and cyclists from many other clubs. In their informal gatherings we hear the usual conversations among those who belong to the fellowship of the wheel: inquests on last week's races, discussions of training programmes; plans for future events; much reminiscence; and a certain amount of criticism of the government of the day, whether in Westminster or the offices of the BCF and the RTTC.

Geoff Mayne with record-breakers Terry Doughty and Barry Minns

CHAPTER 17

In the early season, and especially in the weeks around the Easter holiday, visitors to the Butter Cross Tea Rooms will notice an especial type of racing cyclist. This wheelman will often be past retirement age, though he looks younger. He is lean, wears an ultra-modern road jersey, shaves his legs and has an unusual tan that cannot have come from the pale spring sunshine of north Suffolk. Its not difficult to guess – if you know the sport – that this clubman is a cyclist who has just spent a month in Majorca or one of the other Balearic islands.

Late-winter training holidays have become common in the Godric C.C., as in other clubs. They are now an established part of modern British cycling, which in this way contributes to a wider social trend. Holidays in southern Europe – or even longer sojourns – are easily organised. A person on a pension might find the cost of living less difficult in Puerto di Pollenca than in Bungay. Continental expeditions are now normal for many people over the age of about 60 who enjoy active leisure. Thus it has come about that long warm kilometres on Spanish roads have helped today's veteran racing cyclists to new campaigns on East Anglian courses.

Here are the avant garde of the elderly, leaders of the Godric club in many ways. Veterans of cycle sport enjoy reunions and they also like to race. In 1995 many Godrics joined the 450 people who gathered at Harleston to celebrate the previous 50 years of competition on eastern roads. They had lunch with old friends and rivals. Some of them also rode special time-trials, for their appetite for speed had not diminished over the years. Geoff Mayne was one of them. The Godric club's Chairman was now in his sixteenth year in the veterans' category but could still defeat younger men. In this year he rode a fixed wheel to take the club veterans' 50 record and was also the winner of the Godric vets' all-rounder trophy.

x   x   x   x   x

While praising the veterans, let us also remember the cyclists who had the force of middle age. The 1995 annual dinner was held at the Buck Inn, Flixton. The first of the Godrics to step up to the platform was Terry Doughty, who again received the major share of the club's honours. He was followed by Geoff Reeve. Chris Legood, Kevin Golloghly and Tim Bonnett also won applause for their efforts in the previous year's racing, while Sue Broadbent and Maureen Wigby were first among the 'Godric ladies', as they were still called.

In 1995 even the May Day criteriums had a reminiscent flavour, for they became part of the Bungay VE Day programme. This was a worrying time for the comrades of the Godric club. They had to enquire after the health of Pat Sheppard, who had fallen from his bike on the A143 near Wortwell. He suffered a fractured skull and other injuries. Dean Clarke had also recently crashed on the same stretch of highway. He was one of five or six cyclists who, in that month, had fallen on a road that should have been better maintained. For once, injuries to cyclists had been caused, not by motorists, but by imperfect repairs by the Norfolk County Council. Sheppard's crash was a terrible warning that worse was to come.

The club's events carried on as normal in the mid 1990s, though there was less interest in the grass-track championship. The May Day criteriums attracted crowds of 1500 people, the hill-climb marked the traditional end of the road season and the Broome Heath off-road races entered their thirtieth year. In the winter of 1994–5 the Godric decided to make more use of the club's set of rollers. The idea was to start a roller league. Other clubs who came to Maltings Meadow to race against the Godric were the East Anglian C.C., the C.C. Breckland, the Diss C.C. and the V.C. Baracchi. The Godric usually had two teams in these clubroom events. Prominent riders were Gavin Cole, Terry Doughty, Kevin Golloghly, Chris Legood, John Pugh, Geoff Reeves and James Trenchard.

They were also the club's most active senior riders on the road. And now the start sheets begin to record the contributions made by two veterans who had come to Suffolk from the London area. They were Terry Power and Ron Sutton. Dean Clarke had made a welcome return to racing and found himself in the keen and genial company of Barry Debenham and Graham May. So there were plenty of Godrics, young and old, to vie for the club's many trophies, which at the annual dinner in February 1996 (actually a lunch) were presented by Eileen Sheridan.

As the younger Godrics could not recall, Mrs Sheridan's professional record-breaking career belonged to the seasons between 1952 and 1954. She represented the era in which the Bungay club was born yet retained her cheerful love of cycle sport. Here was yet another example of the long lives and continuity that are part of cycling.

The exploits of older riders were emphasised in the summer of 1996 and the next awards ceremony. Prizes were given to veterans and to one cyclist who came in the new 'super-veteran' category. The vets were Terry Power and Jim Caplin. The super-vet was Ron Sutton, who celebrated his sixty-eighth birthday during the season and also recorded brilliant times in 10s, 25s, a 30 and in the club's championship 50.

The major prize-winner in 1996 was Geoff Mayne, who had forgotten to retire at the end of the previous year and at the age of 58 was as powerful as he had ever been. Mayne set new veterans' records for a 50 (1.57.38), for a 100 (4.8.52) and for a 12 (246.902). He received the President's Trophy for attendances on club runs, the 175 Trophy, the Coles Trophy for winning the club championship 50 for a record eighth time, the Banham Trophy for the vet's BAR, the twenty-first Anniversary Trophy for Most Meritorious Ride of the Year (his 100), the Senior BAR Trophy, the Bezant Cup for the most prominent sportsman in Bungay, together with various other medals and certificates. In this *annus mirabilis* Geoff Mayne finished twelfth in the National Veterans BAR.

Although there was no conscious rivalry between two old friends, Geoff Mayne's excellent season had an effect on John Pugh. He was one of the teenagers who had joined the first Godrics in 1953, and had been in and out of the sport for 45 years. Pugh now began to prove himself the best 'comebackman' in the history of the club. In 1997 Pugh won the Godric BAR and the 175 Trophy. In a full season's racing he went under the hour for the first time and also set the club's veterans' 24-hour record with a distance of 395 miles.

Since he was competing on the rollers in the same week Pugh could be described as both a sprinter and a stayer. His long-distance rides, particularly in 24s, are more impressive. In the day-long race Pugh was able to ride the second 12 hours faster than the first. This is the mark of a great stayer. In 1998 Pugh rode the National 24 Championship, held in difficult and windy conditions. He ran out of time with a distance of 414 miles and was placed sixth overall, the highest position by a Godric in any National Championship. John Pugh's magnificent day and night in the saddle also ensured him first place in the Twenty-Four Hour Fellowship's Veterans' Long Distance BAR.

Meanwhile, and by daylight, the Godric club nurtured the talents of young men who had not ventured beyond shorter distances. In the later 1990s the emerging testers were David Francis, Joe Puttman, Dean Notley and Matthew Sparkes. Two new club members made their talents known. John Dupen was an experienced rider approaching the fortieth birthday that would make him a veteran. Jim Burgess took up cycling while in his early twenties. He rode with great power and panache. In the first 25 of the season Burgess came back to a surprised Doreen Stevenson to take first place with a 59.15. He won many other events and was usually the fastest Godric in 10s and 25s organised by other clubs.

This was the year when the Godric C.C. decided to make the club championship 50 an open event. The 50 was a hallowed race for the Godrics. However, there had never been a large field. Now the forty-fifth edition of the club 50 attracted an entry of more than 70 first-class racing men. They did two circuits of the 25-mile course between Beccles and Harleston. Jim Burgess finished with an electric and muscular 1.59 It was his first ride over the 50 distance. Burgess was supported by David Francis and John Dupen. This Godric trio took the team prize, so the new format of the club's 50 was appreciated by everyone.

Away from the racing scene, the major event of 1998 was the Godric's change of clubroom. The hut on Maltings Meadow had been costly to run, at about £400 a year. The Godric C.C. sold their building to a cricket club for £750 and moved to Bungay High School. There was good sense behind the removal. The club already had good relations with the school, the rent was low, there was more room for the rollers and other equipment, and the Godric now had accesss to a gym and showers.

This deft real estate move was followed by two sponsorship deals. Geoff Mayne agreed a package with the Beccles car firm Warwick Shubrook, thus assuring the future of the May Day criteriums for the next three years. Then the Harleston company PFK Ling – always friendly with the Godric club – matched Warwick Shubrook's generosity with a similar sum to ensure the Cyclathons of the next three years.

In his second year of racing Jim Burgess was again the fastest Godric. His times were devastating but did not completely overshadow under-the-hour performances by John Dupen, and fast rides by 60-year-old Geoff Mindham and Martin Denson, a racing man again after nearly twenty years out of the sport. Shaun Aldous was glad to be back in Godric colours as he sought his first-category licence. Sue Broadbent was always in the placings. The club had a new member with historic connections – Frank Edwards, who in 1953 had ridden in the Tour of Britain. This lively group of riders was joined by Mark Harrison, who won the handicap 25 and at one point in the season achieved three personal bests in the space of five days.

Harrison's rides promised much for the future. There was one sad look at the Godric C.C.'s past. Richard Avery left his home roads for a quite different life in New Jersey. At one of the club's monthly meetings he was presented with an engraved tankard to remind him of his twenty years with the Godric. The former hill-climb champion left England before seeing his clubmates on the new uphill end-of-season course at Gas Hill in Norwich. This was now the venue for an event that was shared with other clubs.

The major achievement of the 1999 season belonged to John Pugh. Now 61, and as voracious a mile-eater as he had ever been, Pugh was regularly riding 1,000 miles a month in training. His preparation gave him 430 miles for a 24, a 246 for a 12, a 50 in 2 hrs. 4 mins. and a 10 in 22.52. These magnificent performances brought him the Bezant Cup as the Bungay area's Sports Personality of the year. This prize was first awarded in 1980. It is noticeable that members of Godric C.C., the representatives of a so-called 'minor' sport, won the Bezant Cup no fewer than six times in the twenty years of the competition. The other winners had been Lindsay Wigby, Doreen Stevenson, Kevin Norman, Julie Smith and Geoff Mayne.

As all wheelfolk know, cycling is not a minor sport. It is, however, a minority sport, in the sense that cycling has fewer participants and spectators than other sporting activities. In 2000, with the golden jubilee of the Godric on the minds of the committee, there were worries that membership was falling and that there was a lessening of interest in the Cyclathon. Terry Doughty organised 'Come and Try It' mountain-bike and off-road races on Outney Common. These events were aimed at school attenders. But Godric recruits were mainly people who had long left school and who found their way to racing through the evening 10s. Membership of the club, as the twentieth century ended, was stable at around 60, seven or eight joining each year, and seven or eight leaving.

Some people were lost to the Godric because they joined other clubs. One of them was Jim Burgess, who saw his future as a member of the Anglia Velo. Others came to the Godric because the club offers such a variety of racing and social events for cyclists of all ages and abilities. Let us take a sample of their activities – between 5 per cent and 10 per cent of the total number of competitive Godric rides – in the years between 2000 and 2002.

A new circuit from Ditchingham to Loddon and Brooke, then back again, made a demanding course of sixteen miles to start the 2001 season. Jim Burgess won, followed by the Godric riders John Dupen, Shaun Aldous, Terry Doughty, Geoff Mindham, Terry Power, Sue Broadbent and Barry Debenham. Broadbent and Debenham would ride a number of two-up races in the next two years. In the club 25 both Broadbent and Terry Power sped to personal bests. The next day Shaun Aldous was in a road-race at Maldon in Essex. Shortly afterwards he had a weekend in which he rode an Eastway criterium in London, then swapped to a mountain bike for a muddy Sunday morning race near Ipswich.

Dean Clarke rode the National 12-Hour Championship (backed by Terry Doughty, in a car). New member John Cooper did a personal best in a 10.

Mike Hudspith went under the hour in the Sudbury C.C. 25 and also shone in the Norwich A.B.C. open 50, as did Geoff Mindham, Barry Debenham and Frank Edwards. Mark Harrison excelled on the rollers, many Godrics went to the carol service at Pulham St Mary, Shaun Aldous won the hill-climb and Frank Edwards won a new prize at the club dinner. The George Stockdale Trophy (a veterans' 175) is now presented in memory of the Godric C.C.'s former President, who died in 2000 after 37 years of wise advice to the club.

In the new year of 2001 another unpleasant sporting course was devised to test the racing members. It was of nineteen miles from Ditchingham, turning at the Poringland roundabout. Mike Hudspith came home first on a 90-inch fixed, a sign that he wanted a serious campaign in the months to come. A few weeks later he was in a Godric team of ten riders who disputed the Great Yarmouth C.C. open 10. Mark Harrison set a new course record in the club 25, Shaun Aldous demonstrated his style in the May Day races, Dean Clarke did a personal best in the Finsbury Park C.C. 50, the Cyclathon raised £3,000 for the British Heart Foundation, roller racing continued through the winter months … and so on.

All these activities reveal a well-organised and versatile club with many active members. The Godric C.C.'s liveliness is remarkable. Yet death comes suddenly to remind the living of the fragile pleasures and interests of life. In the summer of 2002 Keith Stephens of the V.C. Baracchi was killed while racing a 10 on the A143 near Wortwell. As a mark of respect the Godric C.C. cancelled their open 50, which planned to use the same roads on the next morning. Life is more important than cycling.

The death of Keith Stephens on a road so well known to local cyclists darkened the preparations for the Godric C.C.s golden jubilee. Club members shared their sadness with the misery of the bereaved. In a troubled autumn the members of the Godric had never been closer to their Baracchi rivals. No doubt they were guided by the spirit of fellowship that unites all club cyclists. The Godric fiftieth-anniversary dinner was held at the Wortwell Community Centre in 2003, attended by dozens and hundreds of members and friends who stood for the toast 'To the Godric Cycling Club'. It was late in February. The new season would soon begin.

COLES TROPHY
Awarded to the Winner of the annual
Club 50-mile Championship

Presented to the club in 1953 by Mr R. Coles

YEAR	HOLDER	TIME	YEAR	HOLDER	TIME
1953	Barry Minns	2.25.08	1978	Andrew Warne	2.15.32
1954	Barry Minns	2.20.51	1979	Richard Avery	2.08.19
1955	Barry Minns	2.22.55	1980	Dean Clarke	2.11.30
1956	Barry Minns	2.13.57	1981	Kevin Norman	2.03.50
1957	Barry Minns	2.21.08	1982	Kevin Norman	2.03.57
1958	Barry Minns	2.12.31	1983	Kevin Norman	2.08.54
1959	Peter Gilding	2.15.30	1984	Kevin Norman	2.03.10
1960	Barry Minns	2.13.06	1985	Kevin Norman	2.08.07
1961	Adrian Perkin	2.10.58	1986	Richard Cary	2.17.45
1962	Roy Pulford	2.09.40	1987	Richard Avery	2.15.47
1963	John Bunyard	2.06.48	1988	Richard Avery	2.18.27
1964	Geoff Mayne	2.07.37	1989	Jeremy Wentford	2.33.09
1965	John Pugh	2.16.00	1990	Richard Avery	2.21.33
1966	Geoff Mayne	2.15.23	1991	Shaun Aldous	2.10.32
1967	Adrian Perkin	2.04.25	1992	Graham Ward	2.21.41
1968	Adrian Perkin	2.12.48	1993	Terry Doughty	2.06.48
1969	Peter Roe	2.20.00	1994	Terry Doughty	2.12.19
1970	Geoff Mayne	2.09.35	1995	Geoff Mayne	2.07.50
1971	Roly Stevenson	2.16.35	1996	Geoff Mayne	2.05.26
1972	Neil Skipper	2.17.54	1997	Gavin Cole	2.06.23
1973	Adrian Perkin	2.15.16	1998	Jim Burgess	1.59.54
1974	Geoff Mayne	2.13.55	1999	Jim Burgess	1.57.19
1975	Lindsay Wigby	2.18.02	2000	Mark Harrison	2.01.52
1976	Geoff Mayne	2.18.28	2001	Mark Harrison	2.01.52
1977	Geoff Mayne	2.10.51	2002	Mark Harrison	1.59.44

GODRIC C.C. TIME-TRIAL RECORDS

Senior Men

10 miles:	J. Burgess	20.29	1999
25 miles:	J. Burgess	52.24	1999
30 miles:	P. Bedford	1.05.58	1987
50 miles:	P. Bedford	1.52.04	1991
100 miles:	D. Clarke	4.08.47	2000
12 hour:	G. Mayne	252.412 miles	1964
24 hour:	J. Pugh	429.973 miles	1999

Veteran Men

10 miles:	M. Wiseman	21.46	1986
25 miles:	M. Wiseman	54.16	1986
30 miles:	J. Dupen	1.08.03	1999
50 miles:	G. Mayne	1.57.38	1996
100 miles:	G. Mayne	4.08.52	1996
12 hour:	G. Mayne	246.902 miles	1996
24 hour:	J. Pugh	429.973	1999

Senior Women

10 miles:	S. Broadbent	24.13	2000
15 miles:	S. Broadbent	38.58	2000
25 miles:	S. Broadbent	1.04.54	2000
30 miles:	S. Broadbent	1.21.29	2000
50 miles:	S. Broadbent	2.17.06	2000
100 miles:	M. Mayne	4.57.16	1968
12 hour:	M. Mayne	201.412 miles	1968

Juniors

10 miles:	J. Trenchard	21.24	1991
25 miles:	J. Trenchard	54.11	1991
30 miles:	T. Bonnett	1.10.14	1995
50 miles:	S. Aldous	1.59.30	1991
100 miles:	J. Bunyard	4.49.18	1961
12 hour:	J. Bunyard	225.218 miles	1961

Schoolboys

10 miles:	J. Trenchard	21.24	1991
25 miles:	J. Trenchard	54.11	1991
30 miles:	P. Warne	1.23.24	1978
50 miles:	P. Warne	2.20.42	1978
100 miles:	B. C. Minns	5.01.33	1953

Junior Women

10 miles:	C. Smith	25.16	1982
25 miles:	C. Smith	1.07.24	1982
30 miles:	W. Page	1.28.06	1978
50 miles:	B. Grasmeder	2.31.52	1971

Schoolgirls

10 miles:	C. Smith	25.16	1982
25 miles:	C. Smith	1.07.24	1982
30 miles:	W. Page	1.28.06	1978

Senior Men: Tricycles

10 miles:	T. Doughty	25.16	1994
25 miles:	T. Doughty	1.05.47	1994
30 miles:	L. Wigby	1.24.47	1983
50 miles:	G. Mayne	2.17.13	1977
100 miles:	G. Mayne	4.50.24	1977
12 hour:	A. Perkin	232.765 miles	1966
24 hour:	A. Perkin	386.951 miles	1964

Veteran Men: Tricycles

10 miles:	L. Wigby	26.34	1977
25 miles:	L. Wigby	1.08.11	1977
30 miles:	L. Wigby	1.24.47	1983
50 miles:	G. Mayne	2.17.13	1977
12 hour:	G. Mayne	222.138 miles	1977

PLACE-TO-PLACE RECORDS
All are 'out-and-back', starting and finishing at Bungay Post Office

Senior Men

Bungay to Bury (72m)	M. D. Clarke	3.03.04	2000
Bungay to Ipswich (74m)	G. Mayne	3.14.57	1970
Bungay to Cromer (78m)	M. D. Clarke	3.24.08	2001
Bungay to Gt Yarmouth (38m)	M. D. Clarke	1.34.20	2001
Bungay to Aldeburgh (53m)	G. Mayne	2.15.14	1970
Bungay to London (198m)	G. Mayne	9.29.04	1970
Bungay to Kings Lynn (108m)	M. D. Clarke	4.52.00	2001

Junior

Bungay to Lowestoft (30m)	R. Mullenger	1.22.28	1970

Juvenile

Bungay to Beccles (11m)	K. Norman	34.16	1973

Women

Bungay to Beccles (13m)	M. E. Mayne	36.19	1967
Bungay to Harleston (14m)	M. E. Mayne	42.29	1967
Bungay to Halesworth (18m)	M. E. Mayne	52.32	1967
Bungay to Lowestoft (30m)	M. E. Mayne	1.39.05	1967

BEST ALL-ROUNDER TROPHY

YEAR	HOLDER	SPEED	YEAR	HOLDER	SPEED
1958	B. Minns	22.69	1977	G. Mayne	21.991
1959	R. Stevenson	20.489	1978	R. Stevenson	20.464
1960	R. Stevenson	20.251	1979	D. Clarke	20.171
1961	A. Perkin	21.474	1980	D. Clarke	20.89
1962	A. Perkin	21.728	1983	M. D. Clarke	21.896
1963	A. Perkin	22.321	1984	K. Mayne	21.118
1964	G. Mayne	23.069	1987	R. Cary	22.224
1965	A. Perkin	23.033	1988	J. Wentford	20.531
1966	A. Perkin	22.33	1989	G. Ward	18.338
1967	A. Perkin	22.358	1990	G. Ward	19.781
1968	P. Roe	20.675	1992	G. Ward	19.848
1969	P. Roe	21.056	1993	G. Mayne	21.632
1970	G. Mayne	22.432	1995	G. Mayne	22.738
1971	A. Penman	20.699	1996	G. Mayne	23.44
1972	N. Skipper	20.391	1997	J. Pugh	20.70
1974	G. Mayne	22.028	1998	J. Pugh	21.849
1975	L. Wigby	19.724	1999	J. Pugh	22.334
1976	G. Mayne	19.975	2000	M. D. Clarke	23.252
			2002	J. Caplin	16.608